Guide to Godhood
The Roadmap to *Moksha*

Moksha—the State of Godhood, is one of the most mystical concepts of the east. It means rise of an ordinary individual from the realms of manhood into the domain of Godhood. It symbolizes the release of soul from the ever-repeating cycle of birth and death and assimilation of the same into the souls of previously liberated beings, collectively referred to as "Siddha."

This book, "Guide to Godhood—The Roadmap to Moksha," breaks open the path to achieve this high state. It's based on Sutras (verses) of Shraman Theology and divides the journey into Fourteen milestones referred to as "Guna."

Each one of us, irrespective of our beliefs and value system, is stationed at one of these phases (Guna). As a reader reads through the pages of this book, it will not be difficult for him to pin-point the phase at which he is currently stationed. This knowledge of one's current state of being will not only help him analyze where he stands on the spiritual platform, but will also help him in discovering the reason of his stationing at that particular phase and thus plan remedial actions to break free.

The basic idea of this book is to help explain all these phases from a scientific outlook, so a fair idea of the road that lies to Godhood could be achieved.

Amit Jain, the author of this book, is not any spiritual master or a pundit of philosophy and religion. He is an ordinary person, deeply entrenched in the passions and vices which any ordinary mortal experiences and feels. It will not be wrong to say that if a line is drawn between a theist and an atheist, then he is more prone to shift towards the latter.

Born into a middle-class family, he was fortunate to have the best of parenting and schooling. Theology inspired him from his tender age of childhood and reading comics based on this subject was his most favourite pastime. He graduated from Kirori Mal College of Delhi University and did his postgraduation in International Business from FORE School of Management before joining his family business.

As the time passed, his first love of theology deepened further and the comics of childhood gave way to study of scriptures. His modern education and scientific zeal made him look at the Sutras from an analytical sight and what emerged out of it is this book, Guide to Godhood—The Roadmap to Moksha.

The readers are welcome to come and explore. Feel free to leave your comments back at the below facebook page:
www.facebook.com/guidetogodhood.

Guide to Godhood
The Roadmap to *Moksha*
(based on *Shramansutram*)

Amit Jain

Munshiram Manoharlal
Publishers Pvt. Ltd.

ISBN 978-81-215-1263-3
First published 2014

© 2014, **Jain,** Amit

All rights reserved including those of translation into other languages. No part of this book may be reproduced, stored in a retrieval system, or transmitted in any form or by any means, electronic, mechanical, photocopying, recording, or otherwise, without the written permission of the publisher.

PRINTED IN INDIA
Published by Vikram Jain *for*
Munshiram Manoharlal Publishers Pvt. Ltd.
PO Box 5715, 54 Rani Jhansi Road, New Delhi 110 055, INDIA

www.mrmlbooks.com

*To all the Masters
who held my finger . . .
in all the lives I have lived so for*

The realization of "Rareness" of human birth awakens a man. Seeker Amit has tried to bring out the exclusiveness of Jaina School of Thoughts in comparison to others pool of thoughts, which raises the man above the whirlpool of "Birth and Death."

The Fourteen Stages of Human Bhav (phase) has been explicitly explained to lead the human from manhood to Godhood . . ., i.e., "Oneness."

We bless him to elevate internally and externally to finally satiate his quest.

SADHVI YUGAL NIDHI KRIPA

24 April 2013

Contents

Foreword	ix
Preface	xi
Acknowledgements	xiii
Introduction	xvii

1
The Definition of God — 1

2
Fourteen Gunas—Path — 31

3
Stages of Mithyatva—The Legacy of Our Animalistic Past — 39

4
Arrival of Samkit—The Blossoming of Humanity — 69

5
Stepping into Desh Virakt—Declaration of Freedom — 83

6
State of Shramanhood—The Boarding Pass to Godhood — 91

7

Experiences of Apurvkarana—Arrival of ESPs **109**

8

Anter-mhurhat—Last Forty-Eight Minutes to Godhood **117**

9

Keveli—The State of Godhood **153**

Glossary **182**

Index **193**

Illustrations Nine in Colour *facing* p. 196

Foreword

EVERYONE IN THE WORLD wants eternal happiness. Since times immemorial, we have been looking for it. The propagators of different religions have tried to explain the path to eternal happiness—The Path to Godhood, as they experienced the same.

Buddha and Mahavira made serious efforts in search of that bliss and after gaining it, explained in a logical manner. It has been their proclamation that one should not have blind faith. One should logically ponder over spiritual doctrines to find the real truth. Thereafter only, one becomes capable of accepting it and moving ahead on the path.

In this book, *Guide to Godhood*, the author, with his logic and the extensive study of modern science and comparative study of various philosophical thoughts, has tried in a dexterous manner to bring home the uniformity and logic in the basic principles of Jainism. I am sure it will encourage the reader to have a broad outlook in understanding the spiritual concepts and imbibing them in his daily life.

The concept of God and the path that leads to Godhood, has been explained in detail with quotations from scriptures of different faiths. By adding questions at the end of each chapter, the book has become more interesting and thought-provoking. I am sure it will help the reader to develop an interest in understanding the real self—The State of Godhood, and to move ahead on that path to gain the eternal bliss.

RAJ KUMAR JAIN
Retd. IAS Officer

Preface

AROUND TWO THOUSAND FIVE HUNDRED years ago, our planet experienced one of the greatest spiritual revolutions ever witnessed by mankind. It was initiated because of a young prince that the world today knows by the name of Gautama, The Buddha.

Born into a royal family, and fed with every conceivable luxury of the time, He moved on . . ., over a path less travelled, to discover something, which became a beacon of light for generations to come and till date, is one of the most widely read theologies of the world?.

But what made Gautama take that most important step in his life which made Buddhahood possible for Him? What was it, which initiated this young prince, who was heir apparent of his father's kingdom, to renounce everything and move forward?

Legends have it that it was a sight of a monk who appeared completely at peace with himself, which kindled that spark and made him look beyond just the material possessions this world has to offer. The monk belonged to a spiritual tradition called Shraman, which was at the height of its glory during those days.

This book is an attempt to rediscover that tradition and its theology, which must have reached Gautama's ears and made Him take that step—which became a giant leap for Him in discovering His Godhood. This book is a must read for anyone genuinely interested in spirituality as it will transport him into the days, where Buddha breathed and groomed. Hope this book succeeds in preparing the soil for the reader, in which seeds of Buddhahood could germinate.

Because of the great depth and vastness of these *Sutras*, I plan to present them in various volumes, so complete justice could be done to each section. In this volume, firstly we will discuss the meaning of Godhood to explain what this state actually means. Then we will discuss in detail the roadmap which leads to this state and the various milestones a seeker passes through before he completes the journey.

This roadmap called "The *Guna*" (the spiritual stages) has nothing to do with religion or tradition we are following and is completely secular in nature. This is because all of us, irrespective of our believes and value systems, are stationed at one of these *Gunas*. It will not be difficult for the reader to pinpoint the *Guna* he is stationed at as he reads through the following pages.

Love.

AMIT JAIN

New Delhi
1 September 2013

Acknowledgements

THIS IS MY FIRST WORK. Frankly, I never thought I would ever write a book in my life. Nor do I feel, I was capable of doing this. But still, this manuscript happened. It was a more of a happening than doing. It was a result of an overflow of emotions. And help kept coming by, at each stage by itself. I take pleasure to acknowledge a few of them who helped me.

It started with Osho. He was the one who kindled the spark that set me in motion. It was his discourses on the *Sutras* of Jina compiled in his book called *Jina Sutra* that started this process. I was so overwhelmed on reading them that I wanted to share what I gained. And the process of writing this manuscript started.

Having completed my work to the best of my understanding, I went to Ashok Jain, Managing Director, Munshiram Manoharlal Publishers, to help me publish the book. He was very welcoming to the idea but because of sensitivity of the subject, he advised me to get my work approved by some Jain scholars first. He recommended the head of our church, *Acharya* Shree Shiv Muni Ji.

Acharya Shree Shiv Muni Ji is the head of Shwetambara Sthanakvasi Jain tradition. He is very well-versed with English language. However, because of his preoccupations, he could not read my work but guided me to another Jain scholar Munna Lal Ji.

Munna Lal Ji is a noted Jain scholar, teacher of English language and a direct disciple of Osho (Swami Devatithi).

What else could have I asked for! With recommendation of *Acharya* Bhagwan, he went through my manuscript with great care and pointed out my mistakes. He pointed out all the areas where understanding of Osho differed in spirit to the fundamentals of Jainism.

Apart from pointing out all the mistakes, he also made me realize my lack of knowledge about the formulae of *Tatvas*; the centermost principle of Jain Theology.

A special thanks to him for all his help. If it was not for him, this manuscript would never have been what it is.

Next, help came in from illustrious monk Shri Shrayansh Muni Ji. He is a disciple of *Acharya* Bhagwan. He did not read my manuscript, but based on reviews from Munna Lal Ji, he recommended me to do more research on the subject. He made me realize that at that point of time, my understanding was just one-pointed, based on the views of Osho alone, and that doing more research will broaden my point of view and further deepen my understanding of the subject. It was his recommendations that led me to start reading more books on Shraman Theology. It was at this point I realized how naive it was of me to have thought of contemplating on the topic so wide and deep. It was also at this point that I decided to spilt my original manuscript into parts and start moving step by step. That was the time, this first work dedicated to understanding of *Gunas* took its current form.

After having reworked on my manuscript, on a recommendation of a friend, I decided to get the manuscript professionally edited before handing it over for review to eminent Jain scholars. I was introduced to Thejaswini who had an innate interest in the subject and enjoyed helping me put together an edited version free of charge. Her special help is highly appreciated.

Finally, the manuscript started making its way back to the scholars. Munna Lal Ji because of his preoccupation with other works could not spare time and I was on a look out of someone else. Ravindra Ji, a noted Jain scholar came forward to help me and read my manuscript and pointed out a few

Acknowledgements

mistakes. But because of the complexity of the subject, he further recommended it to another Jain scholar, Raj Kumar Ji.

A retired IAS officer and a noted Jain scholar, he is a reservoir of knowledge. He went through the entire manuscript painstakingly and shared with me some more deeper insights on the subject. I was quick to pick up the jewels he imparted me and added them to the manuscript. Furthermore, he along with Ravindra Ji further advised me to get the manuscript approved by some Jain saints and specifically recommended the illustrious Shree Jai Muni Ji Maharaj and highly knowledgable nuns Shree Nidhi Ji and Kirpa Ji.

Disciple of the legendary Shree Sudarshan Lal Ji Maharaj, Shri Jai Muni Ji is a highly respected authority on Jain *Agams*. It was a great honour for me when he accepted to read my manuscript. He critically read through the entire document and painstakingly pointed out my mistakes. The most important being my gross misunderstanding of the state of being at the Eight *Gunas* and the *Kshapak* and *Upsham* directions the seeker takes as he moves ahead on his journey to Godhood. Apart from the above, He also advised me to change my words and presentation of the subject at various places, which I followed in the true spirit of the word. A very special thanks to him for his special help. If it was not for his efforts, this manuscript would have been left with a major flaw.

Illustrious desciples of nun Shri Kaushalya Devi Ji, Nidhi Shri Ji, and Kirpa Shri Ji have authored many books on Jain Theology including the famous *Karam Sahita*. They read my manuscript and blessed me to proceed.

Taking time out by monks and nuns off their daily routine is never easy and I feel greatly indebted to them for having done the same for me. Very special thanks to them for having blessed me with this special favour.

And finally, my manuscript was ready and I got back to

Ashok Jain, Managing Director, Munshiram Manoharlal Publishers. But there was still one hurdle. This revised work was too small to make a commercial book viable. Ashok Ji thus recommended me to add more depth to the manuscript.

This made be get back to the study table and add a discussion section at the end of each chapter. I compiled together the questions which normally get raised when this topic is discussed and put them up together in this section. And the manuscript was ready to go. But before I could proceed with publishing, I wanted to get this new discussion section approved by some masters. The illustrious Shri Dinesh Muni Ji came forward to help me.

Disciple of the Illustrious Shastri Shri Padam Chand Ji Maharaj, he is a shining jewel among the Jain Sthanakvasi monks. He read thoroughly the section of questions and answers and greatly appreciated the queries raised and answered. He also pointed out a few mistakes and highlighted a few areas, where my explanations did not seem entirely in tune with Jain popular beliefs and asked me to mark the same in the manuscript. All His comments have diligently been incorporated.

Finally, the completed and updated manuscript was again read from start to finish by Raj Kumar Ji and he highly appreciated the same. He also blessed me with writing a Foreword for this book. I feel really blessed to have come across him. His special help and support is beyond words to express.

Lastly, I was delighted to get connected with the Facebook page Jain24 and discover their highly descriptive images on Shraman Theology. I found these images perfectly in tune with various chapters of my manuscript and sent in a humble request to use the same. The owners were quick to grant permit along with their blessings.

Introduction

ALBERT EINSTEIN once said, "I do not know if there is rebirth or not, or life after death. But if it's true, then I would like to be born in India as a Jain." [See fn. 31, 41, pp. 180–81] This assertion of the world's greatest scientist towards the world's oldest tradition was not just a coincidence. There is a great similarity between the two. A deep current runs beneath both the institutions. And this current is logic and a deep sense of enquiry into the reason of existence of a particular thing or an object. And this is what makes the Shraman tradition and both its off shoots, viz. Jainism and Buddhism unique.

Unlike other religions which preach to have faith first and promises results later, this tradition promotes enquiry and analysis first and faith later. This spirit of enquiry can be best understood by instructions of Buddha to His followers of not accepting validity of His teachings simply on the basis of their reverence to Him. He instructed that just as a seasoned goldsmith tests the purity of gold through a meticulous process of examination; similarly the seekers should test the truth of what he has said through reasoned examination and personal experiences.[See fn. 32, p. 180]

This reasoning, this sense of investigation is the very essence of Shraman tradition. Thus, it's not a coincidence that a person like Einstein, who was astutely logical in thought and exceptionally high on reasoning, liked this tradition so much that he wanted to explore it being a part of this school.

Putting up the entire Shraman *Sutras* in an understandable format is a mammoth exercise, and is going to take a lot of time and efforts. I am not sure, if I will be able to complete this process in my life span. So I have decided to move in small steps and start publishing my understandings of this subject in small volumes. This book is the first in this process.

God is perhaps one of the oldest words in human consciousness. The First Chapter covers a detailed analysis of what this word means in Indian Theology. A special emphasis has been given to the word *Bhagwaan*. The detailed explanation of this Indian version of God sets the background for a discussion of the path that leads to Godhood. This path is called "Fourteen Gunas".

These the Fourteen Spiritual Stages or milestones a being passes through before it achieves liberation. This is a detailed roadmap of the passage each one of us needs to pass through in our spiritual quest. The Second chapter discusses the same briefly followed by a detailed analysis in balance of the manuscript.

The Third Chapter deals with the state in which a soul arrives in human form after a long process of its evolution. Here we discuss various *Sūtras* associated with this state and understand why a human lives under the spell of this state for long periods of its *Atmic Cycle*. In this section, we discuss the First, Second, and Third *Gunas* (spiritual stages) and the characteristics of the being at each stage.

Then comes the stage where a human achieves humanity for the first time in true sense of the word. In the cycle of its evolution, as the soul gains human form, its mind does not.

Its heart still dwells in the emotions and passions of its long-drawn animalistic past. It is at this point that a human raises a notch above these passions and starts experiencing finer human emotions like love, compassion, and consideration for other forms of being. In the Fourth Chapter, we discuss the Fourth *Guna* (spiritual stage) where this transformation occurs and various *Sutras* that describe the characteristics of a person at this stage.

Gradually, the human says—enough is enough and charts the declaration of its own freedom from all the animalistic instincts of past, and thus sets for itself—its own dos and don'ts. Here for the first time, the human bids adieu to all that is evil in its life and inculcates all that is virtuous. This transformation occurs at the Fifth *Guna* discussed in Fifth Chapter.

Now comes the most important state in the *Atmic Cycle* of the soul. Here the person bids farewell to all those things that tied him into the never ending life-cycle and made him to do actions—both good and bad. At this stage, a person in most likelihood and for its own good, renounces all material possessions and becomes a monk or a nun. This transformation occurs at the Sixth and the Seventh *Gunas* discussed in Sixth Chapter.

As the seeker grows deeper in its self, it taps into the massive reservoir of its hidden capabilities. What emerge out of it are powers, which are often attributed as magical. Today, the modern science calls them ESPs—(The Extra Sensory Perceptions). In this section, we discuss that they are neither magical nor extra sensory. It's all normal as we all have these capabilities inherent in us by birth. The only difference is that we have yet to unravel their mystery. This unravelling happens at the Eighth *Guna* discussed in Seventh Chapter.

Having come so far, all it takes is a perfect spell of Forty-eight consecutive minutes to complete the balance journey. But these Forty-eight minutes may sometime take aeons. Only those seekers are able to make past these Forty-eight minutes, who have perfectly understood and blossomed out of the above lower spiritual stages (*Gunas*). Rest are destined to be doomed back into the starting rungs of spiritual elevation, and forced to relive them. In the Eighth Chapter, we discuss the Ninth and the Tenth *Gunas* which a seeker transcends in these Forty-eight minutes. Here we also discuss the Eleventh *guna* and understand why it becomes the dead-end of the journey to Godhood for those who did not mature completely at the lower spiritual stages.

Those among us, who are able to move past these Forty-eight minutes, then arrive at the Twelfth *Gunas* to discover their Godhood. They break free from the cycle of transmigration of soul and are termed as *"Bhagwaan—The Paramatman"* (The Supreme Soul). This is the highest stage of humanity. We have known such Masters by Arhats, Keveli, Jina, Buddha, and many other names. Such Masters then at the end of Fourteen spiritual stages (*Gunas*), move ahead to become *"Siddhas,"* but leave behind them a beacon of light for the rest to follow. This final transformation of manhood to Godhood takes place at the Twelfth, Thirteenth, and the Fourteenth *Gunas* discussed in ninth chapter.

Each chapter is followed by a discussion section where basic questions which arise at each stage are discussed in detail.

I do not know if Einstein's wish got fulfilled, but this is one simple effort at my end to introduce this tradition to the world. I welcome you all to come explore, enquire, and

Introduction

investigate the depth of truth in this tradition. Be critical as you proceed. Ask as many questions as you wish. The more you enquire, greater you will submerge in this stream; and higher you will rise on the spiritual ladder. I give my email underneath. Please do not shy to ask. I will try my best to answer all the questions. If there are queries beyond me, I will try and get your answers from the scholars of the subject.

With Love
Email: GuideToGodhood@gmail.com   A Seeker, Amit
Facebook: www.facebook.com/guidetogodhood

Guide to Godhood

Definition of God

1

The Definition of God

Sutras

*The Soul is of Three Types,
Bahir-Atman* (Out-bound),
Antar-Atman (In-bound)
and Param-Atman (Supreme-Soul).
Param-Atman is of Two Types—Arihant and Siddha.
—*Samansuttam, sutra # 178,*

Leave Bahir-Atman (Out-bound Soul),
Settle in Anter-Atman (In-bound Soul)
and Contemplate on Param-Atman (Supreme Soul)
by Your Mind, Thoughts and Body.
—*Smansuttam Sutra, 181,*

GOD is perhaps one of the oldest words in the history of human civilization, a word that permeates through every culture and era. This word has had different meanings since the onset of humanity and there are indeed countless philosophies associated with Him.

Most civilizations have referred to God as a Supreme—Superpower which is incomprehensible and unknowable and thus deserve supreme respect. This is very evident in Jewish philosophy. Such deep and mystic is this belief that the most important name which they use to represent God, viz., YHVH is considered as unutterable and ineffable. Thus, most Jews prefer not to write this word, so that it may not ever be defaced or discarded disrespectfully. They consider themselves to be His chosen ones who are supposed to strictly follow His commandments.

As Judaism evolved into Christianity and Islam, this concept of God as A Supreme Entity to be looked on for guidance remained same. This concept is beautifully summed up in the below verses from the Holy *Qur'an*:

> *In The Name of God, The Most Gracious, The Most Merciful.*
> *All Praise is Due to God, The Lord of The Universe;*
> *The Beneficent, The Merciful;*
> *Lord of The Day of Judgement.*
> *You Alone We Worship, And to You Alone We Turn For Help.*
> *Guide us to The Straight Path:*
> *The Path of Those You Have Blessed;*
> *Not of Those Who Have Incurred Your Wrath,*
> *Nor of Those Who have gone Astray.*
> —*The Qur'an*, chap. 1, vv. 1-7

This concept of God is like that of a Fatherly Figure, to whom His children look up to; for instructions and help. Like a father, He is very loving and merciful and bestows favours on His loved ones and promises to stand by them on the "Day of the Judgment". But at the same time, He is also very strict and severe in punishments for those, who disobey the commandments. The same is evident in the below verses of the Holy *Qur'an*:

> *Children of Israel,*
> *Remember the Favors I Have Bestowed upon You,*
> *And Fulfil the Covenant that You made With Me.*
> *I Shall Fulfil The Covenant I Made With You.*
> *Fear Me Alone.*
> —Ibid., chap. 2, v. 40

> *You are Aware of Those Who Transgressed in The Matter of The Sabbath,*
> *Whereupon We Said to Them,*
> *'Be As Apes, Despised!'*
> *We Made Their fate An Example to Their Own Generation*
> *And to Those Who Followed Them*
> *And A Lesson to Those Who Fear God.*
>
> —Ibid., chap. 2, vv. 65–66

Thus, to sum up, this concept of God is a Transcendental Supreme Entity, who is watching our actions and shall punish us or reward us accordingly.

Another idea associated with God is that of someone, who created this world. He was the one, who existed before the creation of this world and He is the one who will supersede it. There is a famous *Sufi* poem that captures this notion as follows:

> *Yeh Zameen jab na thi yeh Jahaan jab na thaa*
> *Chaand Suraj na they Aasman jab na tha*
> *Raaz-e-Haq bhi kisi per ayaan jab na tha*
> *Tab na tha kuch yahaan, tha magar tu hee tu,*
> *Allah Hu.*

(When there was no Earth, and when this Universe did not exist,
When there were no Moon nor Sun nor Sky,
and when there was no obligation of any one towards anybody, When there was nobody.
Even then there were You, only You, Oh Allah!)

Hindus probably contemplated the most on God amongst all civilizations. Their philosophies about God incorporates all of the above, and even transcends them. They coined three different words for God.[2]

The first word for God in Hindu philosophy is *Ishwar*.

Ishwar here is somewhat similar to God in the Jewish-Christian-Islamic philosophy. He is the Supreme Commander—a Super Human, who manages the whole of existence. Just as other philosophies believe that God often sends His messengers or Prophets to convey His messages, Hindu philosophy believes that *Ishwar* takes *Avatars,* i.e. incarnations, to uproot evil and spread His message.

The second word, coined by Hindus for God is *Brahma*. *Brahma* is the one who created this world. He is the one, who is over and above everything. The sole cause of this universe. The one underneath all that exists. *Brahma* is someone that cannot be imagined by the mind, because it is beyond the mind! *Brahma* is the one because of which mind exists, so mind cannot contemplate about Him or describe Him in words. At best, it can just give slight indications about Him. There is a *Sutra* in *Kenopanishad* that states as follows:

> *What one cannot feel with the mind?*
> *But because of which the mind feels.*
> *Know that alone as Brahma,*
> *And not this, which people worship here!*
> —*Kenopanishad,* 1.6

This concept of God superseded the concept of God as someone who needs to be worshipped to seek His blessings and favours or to avoid His wrath. The closest the Western philosophies got to this Indian contemplation of God is in Islam.

What Hindus called Brahma, Muslims referred to as Allah. So close is the similarity between the two that if in the *Upanishads* the word Brahma is changed to Allah, then many hymns of *Upanishads* would look like *Sufi* poetry, and similarly, if the word Allah in *Sufi* songs is read as Brahma, then they would appear to have been inspired by the *Upanishads*.

The Definition of God

The above two poems that we just discussed can be taken as an example. Just read Allah as Brahma in the first, and it would feel like coming straight out of *Upanishads*. Then read the word Brahma as Allah in the second and it would appear as carrying fragrance of the *Sufi's*. This perhaps was the reason that *Sufi's* were so overwhelmingly accepted in India by Hindus. They completely seemed in tune with the Indian traditions and mysticism.

The third word, coined by Hindus for God is *Bhagwaan*. But before we take up this concept of God, we need to discuss another aspect of the two words, *Ishwar* and *Brahma*.

Ishwar, as God as believed by Hindus, Jews and Christians, Some One above, Someone beyond! Similarly, *Brahma* or *Allah*, as believed by Hindus and Muslims, is also—Some One beyond. Both these concepts and all these philosophies of the world believe in some one beyond, *Brahma* or *Allah*, *Ishwar* or God! Any one, but some one—beyond!

These philosophies that have believed in some one beyond have been called philosophies of believers, and these believers have called themselves—Theists.

Now, in every civilization, and in every age, there have been people who have doubted the concepts of God, mentioned above. Such people have been called atheists. Their disbelief in God stems from the question that if there is someone as powerful as God, how is it possible that there is so much misery and sorrow on Earth.

If there is someone called God, then why does He not take immediate action, and punish evil before it raises its head and causes misery for those who believe in Him? How could there be someone called God, who is all-powerful, and still so helpless, so much so that He cannot rescue the ones who vouch for Him.

Therefore, atheists claim that either there is No God, or even if there is some power, then we are not of much importance to Him. Perhaps for Him, our importance is no more than what we give to any microscopic organism. This logic seems very strong because if there is indeed a God, who is all powerful, and an apostle of love and compassion, and still in his rule, there is so much misery as there is today, then this image of God, actually looks very helpless.

The theists have their own answers to these questions. They talk about justice in the other world. They have contemplated about worlds beyond this world, of beautiful heavens with all the possible luxuries that can be imagined in this world—blown to grandiose proportions. And at the same time, they have contemplated about another world beyond this world—Hell, with all the pains and miseries of this world, again blown unto maxima. And they say that those who believe in Him shall get the first, and those who don't shall be thrown into the second.

This raises a lot of hope and fear at the same time, and urges us to accept our miseries today as is, without question so that we could be the first one to reach the "Kingdom of God".

Atheists have always been a strong disbeliever of all this. That's why Karl Marx said "religion is opium". Because such contemplation of religion, takes a person from a state of awareness of his actual state in this real world into—a faux world of hope!

There has been a very strong section of atheists like Karl Marx in India since a very long time. One of their greatest sects was "*Cārvāka*", and they were very strong around 2500 years ago. *Cārvāka*, also called *Lokāyata* (Worldly Ones) was a school of materialists who rejected the notion of an afterworld, the authority of the sacred scriptures, the *Vedas*, and the immortality of Soul. Of the recognized means of knowledge (*Pramāṇa*), the *Cārvāka* recognized only direct perception (*Anubhava*). They advocated a policy of total opportunism and are often described in literature as addressing princes, whom they urged to act exclusively in their own

The Definition of God

self-interest, thus providing the intellectual climate in which a text such as Kauṭilya's *Arthaśāstra* ("Handbook of Profit") could be written.[3]

They believed that there is no God, and that there is no world beyond this one, and that this life is the only one, and thus—Enjoy! Their maxim was not to bother about the other. There is no other, there is no one beyond to question and ask, and there is no state of being beyond this one. They did not believe in the existence of soul. They claimed that just as a betel leaf, when filled with five different types of herbs, leave a red tinge in the mouth, similar is the existence of soul. It's an after-effect of a perfect combination of five materials that make a body. And just like the redness fades away when the herbs are consumed completely, similarly when the five components outlive their use, the soul simply fades away and there is no further existence of the same.

A similar thought has just been proposed by one of the most famous physicists of our times, a modern day *Cārvāka*—Stephen Hawking. He says that "the Brain is a computer which will stop working when its components fail. There is no heaven or afterlife for broken down computers, it is a fairy story."[33]

The Western world today is perhaps passing through the same intellectual revolution that India witnessed in its golden days 2500 years back which dared to question all-prevailing philosophies and beliefs from scientific and logical perspectives. And if this is true, then it means that the West today is most prepared to witness a spiritual revolution on the same scale which occurred in India in its golden days.

The believers of *Cārvāka* were the polar opposites of believers of Hinduism, who were believers of God—either *Ishwar* or *Brahma* or both. Among these two extremes, the believers and non-believers, was another philosophy which rejected both the above theories. It refused the existence of God and also turned down the concept of No God.

This philosophy was not new for India, and its believers trace their roots back to the very beginning of Human Civilization. This school of thought has traditionally been called Shraman, which derives its name from Sanskrit word *shram* which means—Sheer Hard Work.

This school did not believe in the existence of God as a Supreme Commander, and controller of all existence. This school did not believe that this world or humans has been created by anyone or is being controlled by anyone. On the contrary, it believed that this world has always been there and exists because of a universal force of nature rather than anyone's commandment.

The logic behind this belief can be understood by the fact that nothing in this universe exists arbitrarily. All things are related to each other in some way or the other and facilitate existence of each other. Be it the Sun, or Moon, or planets or stars or the mighty galaxies. They all exist in relation to each other. We humans are also a part of this great cosmic structure.

Let's again understand it from another perspective. Can we contemplate the existence of Moon without the Earth? If Earth is somehow taken away from the solar system then what will happen to the Moon? It would lose the bond that ties it to the solar system and it will break free, unless of course it gets into the trap of some other celestial body and becomes a part of its orbit. Similar is the case with us humans. We also exist not because we have been cursed down upon this Earth by anyone, but because we are tied down into this universe because of our bonds of gravity towards different objects of our passions and desires. This bond that ties us back to this universe is called *Jeeveshna* which means desire to live and consume.[1]

Just as the Earth makes the Moon revolve around it, similarly, our respective objects of passions and desires make us revolve around them and keep forcing us to be born again and again. And just as the Moon can break away from the solar system, if the Earth's gravity ceases to affect it, similarly if somehow we humans could break free from the bonds of gravity towards our respective objects of passions and desires, we can also break free from the bonds that force us to be born again and again.

This school puts the entire onus of the existence of man onto himself. Man exists, because of his free will. Man exists because he himself wants to exist, to satisfy his passions and desires. This theory completely takes the role of any third party—of any God out of the preview.

Now this brings us to a very interesting situation. As per this theory there exists mankind and then there exists objects of its passions and desires. And there is no Super Human to moral-police us and check our actions. This means that man is free to do whatsoever he wants. He may go ahead and enter into all those actions that satisfy his passions as long as he is ready to undergo all the pains associated with these actions.

The Shraman School claims that there is no God who will punish man for doing so and he may keep doing whatever he wants, as long as he wants it and both enjoy and suffer its consequences. The second possibility is that man may realize the stupidity of the actions that he undertakes to fulfill his respective set of desires and may break free from those objects of desires.

In the first case, he will keep revolving around his passions and desires and suffer afflictions and in the second case, he would break free and attain a state, where he experiences no strain towards any object or desire and thus experiences a state of liberation.

This school of thought gave complete liberty and independence to man. But at the same time, this school also gave him a great responsibility. It called him the "Creator of His Own Destiny." Someone, who is wholly responsible for his own actions and the rewards and sufferings, arising thereof!

This is a point of great equilibrium. This school of thought frees the man of all fears of a supernatural, superpower who might punish him for his bad deeds or would reward him for his good deeds. At the same time, it makes him responsible for his own actions.

Let's further understand the above difference with the help of an example.[1] Consider a situation where the head of a family dies. Now, the children are free to do what they want. Until the death, they were under the domination of their father and were scared of him. But now there is no one above them to be frightened of. The situation gives rise to two possibilities. The first is that the children may get perverted and start doing all those things that they were forbidden to do in the time when their father was alive and watching their actions. This is where the school of *Cārvāka* would lead to. This is also where the modern, Western thought of non-believers is heading towards that says God is dead—Man is now free to do whatsoever he wants!

The second possibility is that now the children assume responsibility. Now there is no fatherly figure they can rely on, or surrender unto. Now there is no one who would help them or guide them. And now they themselves have to decide their own actions and assume responsibility of the same. Good or bad, pleasure or misery, joy or sorrow. You wish it, you have it.

This second possibility is the very essence of the school of thought called "Shraman."

This school also believed in the existence of the immortal soul and its evolution from the state of *Eik-Indriya Jiva* (Being with just one sense organ like amoeba) to *Panch-Indriya Jiva* (Being with five sense organs, i.e., humans). Their central philosophy is that the soul keeps revolving in different forms of lives, till it takes a human form. And from this point rises three possibilities for it. One is to fall back into the menial state of being, that are beings with one to five sense organs by cultivating his desires and bonds of attraction. The second is to rise above humans, and become a super human or a *Devata* (demigod). The third possibility is to break free from all the bonds of gravity that tie a human to this universe and thus become the liberated one, called The *Bhagwaan*.

This third possibility of becoming a *Bhagwaan* is the third word coined by Hindus for God—the third definition of God. This definition makes God very human. This God is not a super natural super human, but someone among us, someone who is very much like us, but has broken free from all the bonds that we ordinary mortals are tied to and thus has liberated itself.

The above three possibilities are in the hands of the human itself. He may achieve any possibility of the above three by his own will. Until he is human, he is bound by destiny. He will revolve in different forms of life, with little control over its future. But once he attains humanity, he becomes the creator of his or her own destiny, and its progression into higher worlds, or degradation back into the lower ones.

Based on this philosophy, this school of thought divided human soul into three types. First, they called the Out-bound Soul (*Bahir-Atman*), second they called the In-bound Soul (*Antar-Atman*), and the third they called the Supreme Soul (*Param-Atman*) or the soul that has attained Godhood and has raised itself to a state of a *Bhagwaan*.

Jina says:

> *The Soul is of Three Types,*
> *Bahir-Atman (Out-bound), Antar-Atman (In-bound) and*
> *Param-Atman (Supreme-Soul). Param-Atman is of Two*
> *Types—Arihant and Siddha.*
> —*Smansuttam Sutra,* 178

The first, out-bound soul is the soul of the human, who is attached to the outer world, the material world, and its pleasures and sorrows. The second, in-bound soul is the soul of the human, who has detached itself from the attractions of the outer world and directed its energies into understanding and discovering its own deeper realms of existence. The third, The supreme soul is the state of the soul, who has completely liberated itself from all types of gravity towards the objects of this universe and has thus attained the highest possibility of humanity, i.e. Godhood. Such a soul frees itself from the vicious cycle of birth and death.

There is a *sutra* in *Katha Upanishad* that describes this state of being as under:

As Pure Water poured into Pure Water becomes the Very Same,
So does the Self of the Illumined, Nachiketa,
Verily becomes One with the Godhood.
—*Katha Upanishad,* 4.15

Such a state of liberation, where one becomes one with the Godhood and thus breaks from the cycle of birth and death, has been described as *moksha* or *nirvana*.

The followers of this Shraman school of thought devised different techniques and philosophies, to help humans rise above from Out-bound-soul towards In-bound soul and attain the third possibility—The Supreme Soul. These range from techniques of rising awareness through direct perception called *Samyag Darshan* to techniques of extreme austerities called *Tapas*.

Jina says:

Leave Bahir-Atman (Out-bound Soul), Settle in Antar-Atman (In-bound Soul) and Contemplate on Param-Atman (Supreme Soul) by your mind, Thoughts and Body.
—*Smansuttam Sutra,* 181

The Definition of God

This school of thought rose to its highest glory about 2500 years ago, and manifested itself in the teachings of two of the greatest sons of India. One of them *Vardhaman Mahavira*—The *Jina*, rose to become the twenty-fourth and Last Great Master called *Tirthankara* (Ford-maker) of the Shraman tradition, while the other, Gautama—the *Buddha* rose to become the greatest face of Indian spirituality for the entire world.

At heart, there is not much difference in the teachings of these two Great Masters as both of them originate from the same Shraman tradition. In fact, when westerners first started coming to India, they thought both to be same. But they both are different and have proven historical existence. They both lived in the same era and in same area. Such great is the impact of these two masters on the Indian psyche that the area where they both lived and traveled (called *vihar* in local language) is still called Bihar. It was one of the most affluent and intellectually developed regions of India in its golden days and provided the stimulating background for the rise of philosophies like Buddhism and Jainism.

In the following pages, we will be discussing the teachings and philosophies of the first—Vardhman Mahavira—the *Jina*. He is referred to as *Jina* as He conquered the mind and all its desires and thus broke free from all the knots that keep a person tied to this world. He was thirty six years older than Buddha.[21] The *Sutras* that we will be discussing would have been at their height when Buddha was a young man, and should have been one of the most important catalysts in Gautama taking that first step, which made Buddhahood a possibility for Him.

Discussion

- If there is no God, then who created this universe and who governs it?

- If there is no God—The Creator, then how come suddenly in the last couple of centuries has the human population grown so drastically? There must be some power that is creating more souls?
- If soul can neither be created nor be destroyed, but it can escape the transmigration cycle by achieving Moksha! What will happen to this world after all the souls would have achieved Moksha?
- If there exist heaven and hell, and there exists no God, who governs this structure? Who decides which soul gets uplifted to heaven and which soul falls to hell?
- Is it absolutely important not to believe in God to move ahead on the Shraman Path?
- What about The Holy Trinity of "The Father, The Son, and The Holy Spirit"? Does the Shraman Theology believe in it?
- If the State of Siddha is same as that of Father—The God, then can Siddhas be called God?

Question

If there is no God, then who created this universe and who governs it?
As per Shraman Theology, this world is eternal. It was never created, nor shall it be ever destroyed. It existed as is since times immemorial and shall continue to exist forever.

Now this raises some very basic questions as per our current understanding of the universe. The foremost among them is that if this world was never created, then what about the scientific theory of "Big Bang"?

The answer is that scientific community, though in general accepting that Big Bang should have occurred, also claim that this theory is based more on empiricism rather then hard fact. Internationally renowned Astrophysicist George F. R. Ellis explains:

People need to be aware that there is a range of models that could explain the observations. . . . For instance, I can construct you a spherically symmetrical universe with Earth at its center, and you cannot disprove it based on observations. . . . You can only exclude it on philosophical grounds. In my view there is absolutely nothing wrong in that. What I want to bring into the open is the fact that we are using philosophical criteria in choosing our models. A lot of cosmology tries to hide that.[22]

So we need to understand that Big Bang theory is not absolute. There are a lot of bugs in it which have no explanation. And till our scientific community comes up with a reasonable theory of the creation of this universe, the best answer is what the Shraman Theology says—It existed since times immemorial.

The second question is that who governs this universe. The answer is what the modern science says—A Universal Force of Nature. All that we see out there is related and depended to each other. Nothing in this universe, not even a single atom is independent. Each and every thing exists in relation to each other and collectively, they keep the universe operational. Earth ensures that moon keeps in its orbit and revolve. The sun ensures that Earth and all the other planets do the same and do not go astray. And the mighty black hole in our galaxy ensures the same for our sun and for all the millions of stars that we have in our galaxy. And this is how all other galaxies operate. This is how this structure works. This is how it has worked since times immemorial. And this is how it will carry on for times immemorial in future too.

Question
If there is no God—The Creator, then how come suddenly in the last couple of centuries has the human population grown so drastically? There must be some power that is creating more souls?

A soul is neither created nor can it be destroyed. Its one of the six elementary substances that make this universe (*Dravya*) and we will discuss on this topic later in our discussion. Now the question arise that where has these new souls popped up from?

First we need to understand that its not just the humans who have soul. Each and every living being, from microscopic organisms to massive elephants or dinosaurs which once ruled this planet, all have a soul and it transmigrates. And in this process, it evolves into humanity.

So if human population has increased, then it does not mean that more souls have been created. It just means that there are more souls passing through the human form in the current times.

Furthermore, as per Shraman Theology, our planet is not the only one in this universe which supports life, especially human life forms. There are many other planets which do the same. And soul has the capability to travel between different planets in its cycle of transmigration.

Question

If soul can neither be created nor be destroyed, but it can escape the transmigration cycle by achieving Moksha! What will happen to this world after all the souls would have achieved Moksha?

Answering to a similar question by an illustrious princess named "Jyatti" Jina gave simile of Space to explain this equation. Space, as per Jain Theology is one of the six elementary substances that make our universe, and is infinite in nature. Comparing the souls to space, He said that just as if one part of the space is taken out of space, still the space remains infinite; similar is the state of souls. They are infinite in number and thus as one soul breaks free from the cycle of transmigration, the number of soul back in this cycle still remains infinite.

Further explaining this question, some Jain scholar's bank on the most elementary state of existence of soul referred to as *Nigoda*. We discussed earlier that the Shraman school believes in immortal soul and that it evolves from the state of being with just one sense organ like amoeba to a being with five sense organs like humans. The beings with just one sense organ are referred to as beings in the state of *Nigoda* and they are infinite in number and pervade the entire universe.

They are further sub-divided into two types. The first are the beings that are a part of the evolutionary process as they transmigrate. They will by default, sooner or later gain humanity because they are already a part of evolution. The second types are the beings that are not a part of the evolutionary cycle. They do take birth and die, but in this process they do not evolve. These souls act as a reservoir for the souls in the evolutionary cycle. As and when a soul achieves *Moksha*, a soul from this reservoir is released and becomes the part of the evolutionary process. This release is always equal to the souls achieving liberation (*Moksha*). Thus, the number of souls in the universe in evolutionary cycle does not reduce as one of them breaks free.

Since we are already discussing this subject, I would like to point that this state of *Nigoda* is the worst possible state of a being. The religions across the globe have contemplated of heavens and hells in after life. Shraman school also talks of the same, but they are not regarded as much of a virtuous or filthy place as advocated in rest of the religions of the world.

The first reason is that the span at such places is not considered eternal as advocated by other religions. Shraman school advocates that life in these after worlds do come to an end and the being is again born as a human. The second reason is that in both these after worlds, the being does retain all his five senses which he has so painstakingly evolved after a long process of evolutionary cycle.

At *Nigoda*, the being loses these senses and gets diminished back to a being with just one sense organ. Thus, he ends up annihilating all the progress he made and thus it's considered to be the worst place to be as now the being will need to start the cycle of evolution again.

This difference can be better understood by comparing the difference between death penalty and imprisonment. Imprisonment, howsoever long it may be, is not a very good state to be in. But still the person remains intact. As and when the span of imprisonment finishes, the person will be back. But when faced with death penalty, he is annihilated.

Similar is the difference between hell and *Nigod*. Hell may be very painful, but at least the gain a being has made in the cycle of evolution does not get destroyed. At *Nigod*, they do.

This also explains the reason why the forms of life which have five senses are considered exceptionally virtuous and destroying or killing them considered the greatest evil. The being in this state has moved a great deal to be able to achieve it and now deserves to experience the world with them. Apart from us humans, animals and birds also fall in this category. They too have fully evolved five senses. The only difference is that we are a notch higher to them as far as our brains are concerned.

Question
If there exist heaven and hell, and there exists no God, who governs this structure? Who decides which soul gets uplifted to heaven and which soul falls to hell?

The answer is again as before. A universal force of nature ensures it. Let's try and understand it with the help of an example. Say there is a person who is a very good swimmer. He is efficient enough to swim across massive stretches of water. Now consider a situation where a heavy weight is tied onto his back and he is asked to swim. What will happen? Will he be able to swim, or will he sink? The answer is the latter. In spite of all his best efforts, in spite of all his skills, he will sink. The extra weight he is carrying will take him down.

Something similar happens to a being as he accumulates the extra weight of *Karmic* particles (the after effects of good and bad actions we perform). The bad *Karmas* (actions) make him sink into the lower worlds. And the good *Karmas* uplift him to the better ones. This process happens by itself. As a result of the extra baggage, we accumulate in our life times. There is no need of any God to make that happen. The fundamental forces of nature are sufficient to do effectuate it.

Question
Is it absolutely important not to believe in God to move ahead on the Shraman path?

No, not at all! One of the most beautiful concepts of Shraman Theology is its non-absolutism. It says nothing in this world can be said with absolute surety as any statement is true only in relation to the point of view it's quoted for. This should hold true even for this oldest question on existence or non-existence of God.

When Shraman Theology says that there is No God, all it means is that there is no God who created this universe or is the cause behind its creation. When Shraman Theology says that there is No God, all it means is that there is no God who governs this universe and its operations. With No God, Shraman Theology means that there is no God who needs to be worshipped to gain fortunes or avoid His wrath. No God in Shraman Theology means that there is no one above, who is making us move and act like puppets. No God here means that there is no one else who is responsible for our pleasures or miseries.

The idea behind the concept of No God is not to refute existence of God, but to make us take responsibility of our actions and its after-effects—both good and bad. Normally, whenever something good happens to us, we are quick to take credits. We say it's because of our efforts. And when something bad happens to us, we say—"It's an act of God." It's a very amazing statement. You will find it especially in legal contracts. In these legal contracts, the contractor often says that he will not be responsible for any natural calamities like fire, earthquake, volcano eruptions, hurricanes or any other act of God. This statement tends to send a message as if all that is evil in this world—is an act of God.

The societies or people who are more God loving says the opposite thing. Whenever something good happens to them they say it's by "His Grace." And whenever something bad happens to them they say it's a result of their own bad *Karmas* (actions). This is especially true for us Indians. We assume responsibility of all bad things and gives credit of all that's good to the God.

Shraman Theology says both are wrong. Neither does God do any evil, nor does God do any good. All that is good and bad which happens to us, is a result of our own past *Karmas*. It's just like echo coming back to us in mountains. If we shout a dirty word, we will hear that back. And if what we chant a prayer, we will hear that back too.

So, believing or not believing in God is not important. Assuming responsibility is important. As long as we are ready to assume responsibility, it does not make any difference whether we believe in God or not.

When Buddha used to be asked this question, He would just remain mum. He would not answer. Perhaps it was because if He would answer in affirmation, then people would tend to surrender everything to him and escape responsibility. Then they would say—I didn't do it. It happened but for me. God made me do it and escape responsibility of their actions.

And if He would have answered in negation, then perhaps that would not be the right statement. So, He would just remain mum. He was perhaps a true Jew, who thought this subject to be so very pious that even uttering a word about Him would mean sending a wrong message. So, He remained mum.

Thus, to sum up, as per my best understanding, whenever the Shraman school says, "No God," all it wants is to make us mature so we may stop passing the bug, and become capable of assuming responsibility. Only when a person attains this maturity, he becomes capable of mending his actions and tread ahead on the Shraman path.

Question
What about The Holy Trinity of "The Father, The Son, and The Holy Spirit"? Does the Shraman Theology believe in it?

The Trinity of The Father, The Son, and The Holy Spirit is one of the most mysterious subjects of Christianity. It means that God manifests itself in the above three forms. All these three are distinct, yet not a separate entity and exist in unity and are co-equal and co-eternal. This means that they have existed since eternity, together without anyone dependent on the other.

It can be understood better by the below figure:

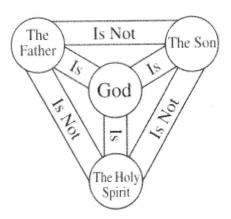

Thus, it tends to lead that there are Three Gods instead of One! For this reason, the entire Christian world is divided into two as this philosophy tends to deviate from their most fundamental principle of—One God.

As far as Shraman Theology goes this formula of Trinity does seems perfectly in sync to their fundamentals. Let's briefly discuss on each of these and their counterparts in Shraman Theology. Let's first start with The Holy Spirit.

The Holy Spirit

It is defined simply as "The Presence and Power of God" which is eternal. The below verses of *Bible* define its properties as under:

> *Where can I go from your spirit?*
> *Where can I flee from your presence?*
> *If I go up to the heavens, you are there;*
> *If I make my bed in the depths, you are there.*
> *If I rise on the wings of the dawn,*
> *If I settle on the far side of the sea,*
> *Even there your hand will guide me*
> *Your right hand will hold me fast.*
> *If I say, "surely the darkness will hide me*
> *And the light becomes night around me,"*
> *Even the darkness will not be dark to you;*
> *The night will shine like the day,*
> *For darkness is as light to you.*
>
> —*Psalm,* 139:7–12

This makes The Holy Spirit an omnipresent force which is all pervasive in the entire universe and a source of guidance for the seekers of the right direction.

There is a reference of a similar force in Shraman theology. It's called *Dharmastikaye,* or popularly just *Dharma.* It literally means—The Virtuous one or the Holy one. Thus, by its very name, it tends to mean the same as The Holy Spirit defined in *Bible*.

It is one of the six elementary substances which make our universe and just like the Holy Spirit above, it's eternal and omnipresent. Moreover, in tune with the reference of The Holy Spirit in *Bible*, it's a force, which comes into action as soon as a being breaks his bonds with the unworthy desires of passion and lust and facilitates its movement to Godhood. From Christian point of view, this facilitation to Godhood can also be termed as "Reunification with the Father."

We will discuss in detail over this concept of *"Dharma"* in Shraman Theology later in our discussion.

But before we proceed, it's important to point that there is one difference between the concept of The Holy Spirit in Christian Theology and the concept of *Dharma* in Shraman Theology. This difference is that The Holy Spirit in the first is considered as a living being, which has a will and can speak. In Shraman Theology, *Dharma* is just a force, which is not living, and facilitates the movement of only those beings who are willing to set aside their passions and desires. It does not force anyone out. It does not motivate any one. A being gets into its virtuous folds as soon as it experiences the uselessness of vices and the afflictions they cause.

Apart from this difference the above two concepts are very similar. They are both eternal, and omnipresent, and facilitate the movement of soul towards the right direction.

The Son

Who is the Son in Christian theology? The following verse from *Bible* explains it:

For All Who are Led by The Spirit of God Are Sons of God.
—*Roman*, 8:14

To understand the meaning of this verse, we will need to

understand one of the basic beliefs of Christian Theology. It is that *Satan* seduced Adam and Eve into desires and passions and thus they were abandoned by God. We humans are their children. Those among us who will break free from these satanic desires and establish themselves in the Holy Spirit will again be reclaimed by God as His sons and will reunite with Him. And this is what's being claimed by God in the above verse. It says that all those beings, who will establish themselves in the Holy Spirit will be claimed back by God as His children.

Shraman Theology does not have any reference of any God abandoning His children as they disobeyed Him, but as far as the reunification is concerned, Shraman Theology does have an exact parallel reference. It says that the very moment we humans break free from our desires and passions to live and consume (referred to as *Jeeveshna*) we establish ourselves in the pious forces of *Dharma*, The Holy Spirit, and start moving towards our destined unification with Godhead. This unification or assimilation of self into the supreme is called *Moksha*.

In the Christian Theology, if a being fails to establish itself firmly in The Holy Spirit, it is destined to suffer in hell till eternity. But in Shraman theology it gets a chance again and again. Even if a being performs such bad actions that it falls in the worst of the hells, still it pops back and gets a chance again. Hell in Shraman Theology is not for eternity. Its phase does come to an end after the being had paid the price of its misdeeds. And after having done so, he again arrives in human form and thus gets a chance again to establish himself in the Holy Spirit and claim his Godhood.

The moment this soul establishes itself in this pious forces of *Dharma*, it's called *Anter-Atman*. And this *Anter-Atman* can be at various stages of unification process with Godhead. It may have just stepped into The Holy Spirit, and it may have already completed the process of unification back with the

Godhead. Thus, depending on their stages, the Shraman Theology divides them as under:

> The seekers which have just entered the Holy Spirit and have recently begun their journey to unification with Godhead are called *Sadhu*". The ones who have mastered the fundamentals of *Dharma* and have achieved the capability of imparting this knowledge to others are called *Upadhaya*. The heads of a group of *Sadhus* and *Upadhayas*— The Pope of their respective sects are referred to as *Acharayas*. These three are all one above the other in the process of unification with Godhead. The ones among us who complete this process of unification are referred to as *Arihants* in Shraman Theology. These are the ones who have completely annihilated the satanic desires and passions and have thus become Godlike but are still bound in their material bodies. From Christian point of view, all the above four can be referred to as "God—The Son" as they all are lead by the Holy Spirit of *Dharma*.

The Father

Who is the Father in Christian Theology? One thing that is important to note here is that it's not what Jews have call, "Yod-Hei-Vav-Hei" (YHVH) or what Muslims call *Allah* or Hindus call *Brahma*. It's because the above three are—"One Single God". These are just different names of the One Supreme Being in three different cultures.

The Father in Christian Theology is not—The One God, but just one part of the Holy Trinity. Collectively, the trinity can be equated to the above, but separately, Father being just one of its constituent, cannot be equated to them. So Father—The God is not "The God" as believed by other theist religions which believe in the existence of "God". Then what is "Father—The God"? And does this concept have any parallel in Shraman Theology?

The answer to the second question is—yes. There is a state of being in Shraman theology that is referred to as—*Siddha*. And there is a remarkable similarity between what Shramans refer to as *Siddha* and Christians refer to as "Father".

Let's try and understand what *Siddha* is and then try and compare it to what is referred to as Father—The God in Christianity.

Siddha in Shraman Theology is the state of a being, which an *Arihant* or some one who has completely annihilated all it's vices as we discussed above, achieves after He leaves His material body. It's the state of someone who has achieved *Moksha* or *Nirvana* and has thus broken free from the cycle of transmigration of soul.

When an *Arihant* leaves His material body, Shraman theology says that it completely merges with the soul of the *Siddhas* of the past and loses its individuality. It now becomes *Siddha—The God*. From Christian point of view, it can be understood as "Reunification of Son with the Father."

Now let's try and discover if this concept of *Siddha* has any similarity with what is referred to as "Father" in The Bible.

Bible states:

I And The Father Are One.

John 10:30

In this verse, Jesus says that He (The Son), and Father— The God are one. This is completely in tune with the concept of *Arihant* (The Son) living in His material body and *The Siddha*.

Jesus claim that His state, i.e. the state of The Son who is so firmly established in the Holy Spirit that all His vices have annihilated and thus become worthy of assimilation in the Godhead (which is the state of an *Arihant*), is the same as the state of the Father above, i.e. *The Siddha*.

The Definition of God

Jesus further claims:

> *If You Know Me, You Will Know My Father Also;*
> *And From Now On You Have Known Him and Seen Him.*
>
> John 14:7

This claim again seems perfectly in tune with the Shraman theology. Because knowing the *Siddha* is not possible! It's a state of *Nirvana*. And the only glimpse of that state we can have is through knowing the *Arihants*.

At another place, Jesus says:

> *Do you not believe that I am in the Father, and the Father in me?*
> *The words that I say to you I do not speak on my own authority;*
> *but the Father who dwells in me does his works.*
>
> John 14:10

And this is how says the Shraman Theology that the *Arihants* derive their knowledge from. They do not speak anything on their own, but just reinitiates what they have known as a result of their connection with the supreme knowledge. This is the reason that the teachings of all the Twenty-four Great Masters of Shraman Theology called *Tirthankars* were perfectly in tune with each other.

Yet another startling similarity between The Father and *The Siddha* is the below verse:

> *The Father judges no one but has given all judgment to the Son,*
> *so that all may honor the Son just as they honor the Father. Anyone*
> *who does not honor the Son does not honor the Father who sent him.*
>
> John 5:22-23

Jesus says that honoring The Son is as important as honouring the Father because anyone who does not honour The Son, does not honour The Father. This is exactly how Shramans perform their prayer. In their greatest *Mantra*—

The Namokar Mantra, The Arihants are paid the homage first and *The Siddhas* next.

Another revelation which the above verse makes is that *"Father Judges No One"*. This statement makes this concept of Father—The God completely different from the concept of God in rest of the religions. This is because every other religion says otherwise. Every other religion says that God is very stern and strict in punishing the evil.

But at the same time this statement makes Father—The God completely in tune with the state of *The Siddha* in Shraman Theology. This is because Sharmans claim a similar "no-judging" state for *The Siddhas*. This theology says that *Siddhas* are *vit-ragi,* i.e. beyond all bonds of love and affection. So they do not judge anyone. They cannot be pleased by offering prayers. Same way they do not get annoyed either by abuse. They are just beyond all judgments.

Thus, citing the above verses, it can easily be established that what Jesus referred to as "Father—The God", is the same force, the same being which the Sharmans have called *Siddha*.

Besides these similarities and parallels between the Shraman and Christian schools, there is another major similarity between the two. Its in the way they offer their homage. Christians offer their homage to The Son and The Father alone. They do not offer any homage to the Holy Spirit,[42] which is rather strange. This is because they believe that the Holy Spirit, like the Son and the Father is a living being. If its living, and being an equal member of the Triune, it should command the same respect. In fact, just as the Father cannot be given due respect without respecting the Son, as it's the Son that leads to the Father, then following the same logic, the Holy Spirit should also be respected, as it's because of this virtuous force that a person connects with the Son, and itself becomes capable of being called a Son.

Nonetheless, it brings forth another remarkable similarity

with the Shraman school of thought as in this school too, it's just the Son's and The Father that take all the credits.

In their greatest *Mantra*—*The Namokar Mantra* which we referred earlier too, after paying homage to The Sons (*Arihants*) and The Father (*Siddhas*) the next three homages are paid to the *Acharays* (The Son's who are popes of different sects of Shraman school) followed with homage to *Upadhayas* (The Son's who impart the sacred knowledge to other's) and then to *Sadhus* (The Son's who are established in the Holy Spirit).

The Holy Spirit—The pious forces of *Dharma*, which carries the being from the state of a no-son or a sinner to the state of an *Arihant* (The Perfect Son), doesn't get any credits because its considered non-living—just a force without any will or consciousness.

This remarkable similarity between the Shraman school and the Christianity cannot just be a coincidence. There has to be a deep connection between the two. We will discover this connection later in our discussion.

Question
If the State of Siddha is same as that of Father—The God, then can Siddha's be called God?

Yes. *Siddhas* are called God in Shraman Theology. But as we discussed at the start of this discussion, unlike The God in Jews, Muslims and Hindus, and to a great extent the Triune of Godhead in Christianity, *Siddhas* are not considered as the creators of the universe or the ones who manage it. It's just a state of a being who has transcended all vices and have thus perfected itself and broken free from the never ending cycle of transmigration of soul. It's the State of *Moksha*. It's the state of perfect bliss called *Nirvana*.

Fourteen Guna's—The Path

2
Fourteen *Gunas*—The Path

Those States Resulting From the Fruitation etc. of Karmas (Actions), By Which Souls Are Distinguished, are Given the Name "GUNA" (spiritual stages) By The Omniscient.
—*Smansuttam Sutra,* 546

There are Fourteen Guna (Spiritual Stages)
In The Path Of Gradual Spiritual Development:
(1) *Mithyatva* (State of Wrong Belief),
(2) *Sasvadana* (State of Failing from Right Belief),
(3) *Misra-bhava* (State of Mixture of Right Belief and Wrong Belief),
(4) *Avirata Samyag Drishti* (State of Conscious Uncontrolled),
(5) *Desh Virakt* (State of Defining One's boundaries),
(6) *Pramat Virakt* (State of Subconscious Uncontrolled),
(7) *Apramat Virakt* (State of Subconscious Controlled),
(8) *Apurvakarana* (State of Never before Experiences)
(9) *Anivrttikarna* (State of Constant Thoughts),
(10) *Suksham Sampray* (State of Reflexes Uncontrolled),
(11) *Upshant Moh* (State of Dormant Desires)
(12) *Kshin Moh* (State of Transcendence of Desires),
(13) *Sayogi Keveli Jin* (State of The Supreme Soul with Body),
(14) *Ayogi Keveli Jin* (State of *Moksha* or *Nirvana*)
—Ibid., 546–47

HUMANITY IS THE highest form of evolution of soul that our planet is capable of experiencing. As discussed earlier, this evolution starts with a stage of *Eik-Indriya Jiva* (Being with just one sense organ like amoeba). Gradually, our senses develop and evolve. During this process, we pass through various forms of life like plants, insects and animals. Finally, as the senses fully evolve, we take a form of a *Panch-Indriya Jiva* (Being with five sense organs), i.e. humans,

Let's name this process of evolution of soul as *Atmic cycle*. *Atma* means soul, so this term means cycle of the soul. After the soul or subtle mind in the process of evolution, takes a human form, a whole new chapter opens in its *Atmic cycle*. This fully evolved mind now becomes capable of experiencing the fourteen stages we will be discussing in this chapter.

These fourteen stages are a very minute and detailed explanation of the state of a human mind and explain the various phases a soul passes through towards its progression to Godhood. As a starting point, it arrives in the first stage. And then gradually, depending on its actions, move forward or backward. As a human, we all are at one of these stages. As a human in this life, or in past lives, we could have experienced many of the higher stages we will discuss ahead. It's important to pinpoint the stage that we are currently at. This will help us understand the road we need to tread as we move forward.

The above *Sutras* are one of the later Sutras in the Holy Book *Saman Suttam*. But I have decided to take them as number one, as this *Sutra* shows us the complete road map. This complete knowledge of various stages we have passed through, or will pass through in our gradual evolution is very helpful in deciding ones own state of being and in deciding ones own future course of action.

Another thing that one needs to keep in mind is that these stages have nothing to do with Shraman tradition or school of thought. One does not have to be Shraman to experience it or understand it. It's completely secular. Irrespective of our believes and value systems, we can easily understand the logic in these fourteen stages of soul and appreciate the changes which happen in the mindset of a seeker as it evolves and raises at each stage.

For the ease of understanding of each stage, I have marked in bracket a brief description of the state of mind of the seeker at that stage.

It's just for the ease of understanding. It should not lead to a misunderstanding that the fourteen *Gunas* are the fourteen states of mind. This is because *Gunas* are not the state of mind, but the state of the soul. The mindset of the person is just the reflection—the shadow of what the soul is passing through.

The names of these stages and the brief description of the mindset of the person at each of these stages are as under:

(1) *Mithyatva* (State of Wrong Belief)
(2) *Sasvadana* (State of Failing from Right Belief)
(3) *Misra-bhava* (State of Mixture of Right Belief and Wrong Belief)
(4) *Avirata Samyag Drishti* (State of Conscious Uncontrolled)
(5) *Desh Virakt* (State of Defining One's boundaries)
(6) *Pramat Virakt* (State of Subconscious Uncontrolled)
(7) *Apramat Virakt* (State of Subconscious Controlled)
(8) *Apurvakarana* (State of Never before Experiences)
(9) *Anivrttikarna* (State of Constant Thoughts)
(10) *Suksham Sampray* (State of Reflexes Uncontrolled)
(11) *Upshant Moh* (State of Dormant Desires)
(12) *Kshin Moh* (State of Transcendence of Desires)
(13) *Sahyogi Keveli Jin* (State of The Supreme Soul with Body)
(14) *Ayogi Keveli Jin* (State of *Moksha* or *Nirvana*).

These stages keep changing moment to moment depending on the actions of a person.

Now let's discuss each of these stages in detail. For the ease of understanding, we will be discussing these stages in seven subsets. This grouping is just for our understanding so we can easily recognize the difference in the characteristics of the being as it flows through these fourteen phases of its *Atmic cycle*.

Discussion

- The *Gunas* are the stages a soul passes through till it achieves *Moksha* (Godhood). But Buddhism, the biggest branch of Shraman Theology, does not believe in existence of Soul. Does this mean they do not acknowledge these fourteen *Gunas* (stages)?
- If these fourteen stages are secular, and open to all humanity irrespective of believes or values systems, then why is such an importance given to taking refuge in the *Sangha* (The commune).

Question

The Gunas are the stages a soul passes through till it achieves Moksha (Godhood). But Buddhism, the biggest branch of Shraman Theology, does not believe in existence of Soul. Does this mean they do not acknowledge these Fourteen Gunas (stages)?

I would again like to reiterate that the fourteen *Gunas* are not something to be believed in. It's something that is. It's existential and thus need logical analysis and not belief. It's just like any other scientific principle. Something that is to be understood as it takes place. Say, for example, the fundamental that water evaporates at a 100°C and freezes at 0°C. The water does not need to believe that it will evaporate or freeze at these temperatures. It just happens. Same is the case with these fourteen *Gunas*. They just occur to us, irrespective of the fact whether we believe in them or not.

It's got nothing to do with Jainism. We do not need to be a Jain to pass through them. We all, irrespective of our beliefs, or value systems, does exist on one of these fourteen places and shall pass through them as we move ahead on our spiritual quest.

Now let's get to the question of Buddhism and its believe in non-existence of soul.

It's true that Buddhism does not believe in soul. But it does claim that the being transmigrates and that there is a way to break free from this cycle of transmigration and achieve *Moksha*.

Now the question that arises here is that if there is no soul, then what is it that transmigrates? It certainly is not the material body, as the material body gets destroyed at death? Now if there is no soul, then there should also be no transmigration.

The answer to this question which the Buddhist masters give is that it's the "Subtle Mind", which transmigrates. They say, when the body is destroyed at death, the subtle mind escapes, and based on its good or bad deeds, is re-born into another form. Thus, though they do not believe in soul, they do believe in something which is beyond the material body— our real self. Thus, from this angle, as far as transmigration of our real self is concerned, both the branches of Shraman school do agree on the same and thus the Buddhists should not have any difficulty in accepting the fourteen *Gunas* through which this real self—Subtle mind—passes through as it moves towards *Moksha*.

As we move ahead on our discussion, and discuss each of these fourteen stages, it will not be difficult for us to point a parallel between the condition of soul at each stage and the state of our mind at that stage. They would seem to move hand in hand. This will further help us understand that what Buddhism refers to as "The Subtle Mind", is same as to what rest of the religions of the world have called "Soul".

Question

If these fourteen stages are secular, and open to all humanity irrespective of believes or values systems, then why is such an importance given to taking refuge in the Sangha (The commune)?

Sangha is referred to as a communion of masters and disciples on the path to spiritual elevation and is regarded as a great virtue. But taking refuge is not a precondition to achieve or experience the heights of spiritual elevation. After all *Jina* did not join any *Sangha* (commune) and still discovered His Godhood. Buddha did join various ascetic orders of His time, only to abandon them and finally discovered His Godhood on his own.

Thus, joining a *Sangha* (commune) is not important. The question which now arises is then why such a great importance is given to taking refuge in the same? Why is it regarded as a great virtue?

Perhaps the answer is that it just makes the journey to Godhood a lot easier.

Let's try and understand it by taking an example. Say we need to travel from a point called A to point called Z. We have never travelled this road before and are completely unaware of the way. Now there are two ways to complete this journey. First is, we move on our own. We have faith in ourselves and our ability to find our way. As long as we keep moving, we will definitely complete the journey.

The second is we take help of someone who has seen the way or resort to a GPS navigation system. Those among us who have used it to travel in unknown territories would know what a marvel of technology GPS is. Well before a turn needs to be taken, it informs us. The best part is if we go astray, it immediately recalculates and puts us back on right path.

The *Sangha* (commune) does the same for us on the spiritual path. It's a journey, we need to travel alone. There is no one who will move along with us. But being a part of the commune, there are always friends around to guide us and warn us whenever we go off track. And that makes a great difference. With help around, the journey becomes easy.

And that's what makes this communion a great virtue. That's why Buddhist says *"Sangham Sharnam Gachhami"*. It means I am going in the rescue of the commune. That's why the Jains says *"Keveli-Panattam Dhammam Sharnam Pavajjami"*. It means I come to the refuge of the path set by the Enlightened Masters. And that's the only difference.

Moving alone, a seeker will have to make out its own way. In communion, the seeker just needs to walk the path already set by the masters.

Moving alone, a seeker can also reach and experience the same heights of spiritual upliftment as the one who is in a *Sangha* (commune). All that he needs is a sheer will to move and an intellect, that is capable of knowing what's good and what's bad. That's all that is required.[34] This intellect is referred to as *Pragya* in Shraman Theology. It's a state of mind, which having understood that something is unworthy does not perform that action. Say for example once we know that fire burns, we will not attempt to touch it. Similarly, someone who is well settled in *Pragya*, keeps leaving unworthy actions and keeps moving ahead on the path to enlightenment even without any communion of a master.

And a seeker who takes recourse in the *Sangha*, gets the guidance of his peers in understanding the hollowness of unworthy actions and tread the same path.

However, it's worth noting that it does not mean that *Pragya* is not required on taking recourse in the *Sangha* (commune). As we will move ahead, and discover higher *Gunas* (spiritual stages), we will discover that after reaching a high stage in spiritual elevation, the *Sangha* (communion) ceases to be and it's only the *Pragya* of a seeker that steers its way forward. If one is to be chosen between the two, the *Pragya* is a higher virtue. But if one gets the benefit of both *Pragya* and the *Sangha*, then certainly, it's better. Its like getting the best of both worlds. That's why taking refuge in a *Sangha* (commune) is given a great importance in the Shraman School.

Stages of Mithyatva—The Legacy of Our Animalistic Past

3

Stages of Mithyatva—The Legacy of Our Animalistic Past

Not Having Complete Faith in Tatva's (elements) is Mithyatva.
Its of Three Types viz. Abhigrahik, Anabhigrahik & Sanshayit (doubt).
—Smansuttam Sutra, 549

A Soul, Sometimes, After Having Achieved Great Heights of Right Belief,
Still Falls Back Into State of False Belief.
But Has Yet Not Fully Entered the Wrong Belief.
Such A Mid State Is Called Sasvadana.
Ibid., 550

The Mixed State of Right Faith and Wrong Faith,
Which Can, in No Way be Split up Into Two.
It's Just like a Mixed Taste of Curd and Treacle (form of sugar) Which can not be described as Sweet or Sour.
Ibid., 551

HERE WE WILL BE DISCUSSING the first three Gunas (spiritual stages).

1 *Mithyatva* (State of Wrong Belief)

The *Sutra* places this state at the lowest ladder of human existence. It's a very complex word and has a lot of dimensions. I will try and highlight all of them one by one. To start with, it's a state of a person who is totally ignorant of the higher possibilities of existence that he can achieve. This ignorance results in his getting tied down into the material world.

The most common word that is used in Jain annals to describe this stage is *agyan* which literally translates into "No-knowledge". The word Buddha used to describe the similar state of a being is *avidhya* which also means "ignorance or lack of knowledge."[6]

A person at this stage, because of his lack of knowledge, is not able to distinguish between right and wrong. As a result, he is not able to judge as to what is worthwhile for him and what is futile which further results in him getting absorbed in unworthy actions under the influence of his desires and passions. Buddha also said that it is a lack of knowledge that leads one into unworthy actions and it is the Right Knowledge that leads one into worthwhile actions.

Thus, from this angle, *Mithyatva* can be described as a state of faulty sight resulting out of lack of knowledge and drenched in one's bonds of love and passion.

This faulty sight further leads a person into accepting that his prejudiced point of view contaminated by his bonds of love and passions is the only correct one and that all other point of views are wrong. Such a state of mind has been described in Jain annals as "*eikant-vaad*" or one-sided point of view. Such a person totally rejects views that tend to, or appear to be even slightly different to what he believes and becomes fanatic towards his own set of beliefs. Such a person then develops a very rigid mindset and becomes inflexible. Buddha used to say "I don't envision a single thing that, when undeveloped, is as unpliant as the mind. The mind, when undeveloped, is unpliant."[35]

Thus, from the second angle, *Mithyatva* can be described as a state of mind that is fanatic or rigid in nature. This unpliant and fanatic stand then leads a person into accepting all that he has been conditioned into accepting as correct without actually analyzing the logic and truth behind them.

Stages of Mithyatva—The Legacy of Our Animalistic Past

Such a state of mind has been referred in Jain annals as *vanyik*, where one accepts all traditional facts, beliefs, rituals, and rules without applying intellect.[6]

From this angle, *Mithyatva* can be described as a state of mind that accepts all that it has been told of, without understanding the reason or logic behind them.

Collectively, the above faulty visions further leads a person into a state of mind that is referred to as *Abhigrahik Mithyatva* where one becomes fanatic about accepting just his own beliefs as true and rest everything as false without any logical thinking behind it.

Thus, to sum up, *Mithyatva* in its *Abhigrahik* form can be best described as a state of mind with a faulty sight, which due to lack of knowledge and prejudiced by its bonds of love and passions, results in accepting a certain philosophy as the sole truth and thus succumbs into accepting all its rituals, traditions, and rules without intellectually evaluating the logic and science behind them.

The cornerstone of such a faulty sight is perhaps the fact that one's attachment to one's own beliefs is so deeply rooted in one's psyche that this bond of attachment itself prevents one from accepting that anything could even be equal if not better than one's own. Say, for example, a Muslim comes to a Christian and says that Prophet Mohamed is the last prophet of God. He is over and above Christ. Then the Christian ego is bound to be hurt and he would immediately want to reject Prophet and all his teachings, without even understanding what He stood for. Similarly, a Muslim would feel like rejecting all theories or philosophies that stood before Prophet or came into existence after Him, claiming all else is false or outdated.

A few years back, I met a Muslim scholar. I like to know about different religions and this led me into a discussion of Islam with him. During this discussion, he came out with a very good simile. He said that just as when Microsoft launched

Windows Vista then all the previous versions of Windows became outdated, the same is the case with Islam. When the good Lord sent over His last Prophet, all the teachings of the previous Prophets became outdated and were unworthy of a second thought.

It makes sense that when a new version of software is available, then it is stupid to consider previous versions. However, perhaps religion is not as simple as software. Following the logic of my Muslim friend, I asked him whether since Guru Nanak came later than Prophet Mohamed, His teachings should become the latest version of the Message from Beyond? The answer was—No.

Religious beliefs come packed with more subtle emotions. One's ego is also attached with one's religion. Perhaps on a religious point, when a person claims "I am correct", it's not as much about the religion or point of view that he is actually claiming as correct, but more about "I". It's more about his ego. It's not about whether his religion is correct, but about how could he be wrong? If a person is Hindu, then Hinduism has to be correct because otherwise, his ego is hurt. And differences in religions and beliefs are sometimes so startlingly huge, that its hard to accept that both could be true at the same time.[1] The same is true for followers of all other religions. This staunch belief is called *Abhigrahik Mithyatva* which leads one to deliberately reject all opposite theories or philosophies.

Another aspect that is often used to describe the state of *Mithyatva* in Jain annals is *viprit-gayan* which translates into opposite knowledge. This also results out of one's prejudiced sight infected by one's bonds of love and passions. Because of this biased outlook, one starts believing unworthy things as worthwhile and worthwhile things as unworthy. In Jain annals, such a person is described as having a faulty sight where he starts to believe:

—*Jiva* (Soul) as *Ajiva* (non-Soul)
—*Ajiva* (non-Soul) as *Jiva* (Soul)
—Consider the right path of spirituality as the wrong path
—Consider the wrong path as the right path of spirituality
—Consider the right path-following monk similar as one following the wrong path
—Consider a wrong path-following monk similar as one following the right path
—Consider the path of worldly life as the path to liberation
—Consider spiritual path to liberation as a wrong path
—Call liberated souls as non-liberated souls
—Call non-liberated souls as liberated.

Buddha also referred to a similar set of beliefs that lead to spiritual destruction of a seeker. They have been complied in the Buddhist holy book of *Anguttara Nikaya* and are as under:
spiritual actions as non-spiritual
non-spiritual actions as spiritual
monk mis-rules as monk rules
monk rules as non-rules
words not spoken by Buddha as Buddha words
words spoken by Buddha as non-Buddha words
non-actions of Buddha as actions of Buddha
actions of Buddha as His non-actions
rules not made by Buddha as made by Him
rules made by Buddha as non-rules
non-guilt as guilt
guilt as non-guilt
small guilt as big guilt
big guilt as small guilt
serious guilt as non-serious guilt
non-serious guilt as serious guilt
non-specific guilt as specific guilt

specific guilt as non-specific guilt
forgivable actions as not forgivable
non-forgivable actions as forgivable.
To sum up, they all mean distorted knowledge.

Such a state of mind is refereed to as *Anabhigrahik Mithyatva* and results in equating unworthy things to worthwhile and vice versa. This should be specially understood in comparison to *Abhigrahik Mithyatva* that we discussed above. *Abhigrahik Mithyatva* starts as a result of no-knowledge or deliberate rejection of knowledge resulting in a person getting fanatic about his own views without intellectually analyzing them. While under *Anabhigrahik Mithyatva* a person is secular enough to consider and understand alternate theologies but still because of lack of proper knowledge, cannot evaluate them accurately and thus equates unequal things at par or improper things as proper.

The third dimension of *Mithyatva* is doubt. It's different from the *Abhigrahik* and *Anabhigrahik Mithyatva* we discussed above. Such a person is open to understanding alternate theories or philosophies, but still is not able to accept them in spite of seeing a glimpse of truth in them. Together these three constitute the three types of *Mithyatvas* or states of wrong belief.

Before we proceed further, let's consider why a human lives under the spell of this state. Let's first start with doubt! Why does a person doubt when he is told of something new even when he sees a glimpse of truth in it? There could be many reasons. It's not easy for a human being to believe in any new theory or ideology even if they see a glimpse of truth in it.

This is because with the change in theology changes the terms defined for the Supreme. For example, *Brahma* gets replaced with *Allah* and so on. This different terminology, and the difference in its description, creates a lot of confusion and suspicion.

Furthermore, religion is not just a source of spiritual upliftment. It is also a source of great faith and assurance that there is someone above who takes care of us. Accepting any new name, or methods or ideology, also creates fear that the one in whom we believed so far may get annoyed. We humans are cowards by nature. We usually walk in herds. We feel safe in doing so. So we prefer to sit back, in the society or peers, we are currently living with, in spite of seeing truth in someone opposite to us. The logic we give to explain our action is doubt. We say we are not sure if someone, not one among us, or not saying exactly what we stand for, or even standing opposite to us, actually knows what he pretends to be saying he knows. But this is just a façade, to escape taking responsibility. We are actually frightened.

Now lets consider *Abhigrahik Mithyatva*. There are two reasons of why a person lives under this spell. First is lack of knowledge of the Right Path of spirituality. Since he has never been told the higher forms of existence possible for him, he continues to live under this spell. A soul in its *Atmic Cycle* arrives in the human form in this state. It can easily be moved ahead from on acquiring the knowledge of higher realms possible for him.

The second reason of a person living in *Abhigrahik Mithyatva* is a state of mind, where one deliberately rejects the theories or philosophies that can lead one to higher realms of humanity. Now why would anybody do that? There could be personal reasons. The truth might go against his personal interests. In Islam, such people have been called *Kafir*. The term, *Kafir*, was used to describe people who knew The Prophet and His message as well as they knew their own sons, but concealed this fact because it did not suit their commercial and political interest.[7]

This was perhaps the reason why Jesus was crucified or Socrates was made to drink poison. This was perhaps the reason why *Jina* and Buddha were ridiculed. The people who did so were not necessarily their opponents in faith. They probably did so deliberately to safeguard their own political and commercial interests.[1]

This is the second reason of a person living in the state of *Abhigrahik Mithyatva* or wrong beliefs—deliberately rejecting the truth, for their own personal interests.

The last type of *Mithyatva* is *Anabhigrahik Mithyatva*. Here, a person equates unequal things as equal or unworthy things as worthwhile. The reason is lack of complete knowledge. Such a person would automatically move out of the unworthy things, as he explores more about truth on his own accord and with his intellect. This perhaps is the last phase of *Mithyatva* a person passes through on his way out to higher realms of spirituality.

Together, these three types of faulty sights have been summed up in the below *Sutra* as under:

Not Having Complete Faith in Tatva's (elements) is Mithyatva.
Its of Three Types viz. Abhigrahik, Anabhigrahik & Sanshayit (doubt).
—*Smansuttam Sutra*, 549

A very important word comes up in the above Sutra. This is *Tatva* (elements). *Tatva* is a very special term and is the cornerstone of entire Jain theology. It defines various substances that constitute this universe and their relationships. At this point it's too early to elaborate on it, but we will discuss on this topic later in our discussion.

2. *Sasvadana* (State of Failing from Right Belief)

This is a very special state of a soul or subtle mind. All the other spiritual stages are experienced as the soul rises on the spiritual ladder, but this stage is experienced as the soul falls down from the higher levels of existence on the way back to the first stage of *Mithyatva*. During this process, the soul experiences a slight glimpse of Right Insight—a state which a soul experiences only in very high realms of spirituality. However, this is only for a very short duration and the soul then falls further into the first stage. It can be better understood taking the example of a vomiting person. Just as while vomiting, a person tends to experience a taste of all that he has been consuming, similarly, during his elevation on higher levels since the person has been consuming a lot of spirituality, during his fall, he tends to experience a state of a spiritual high which lasts only for a very short duration.

The *Sutra* that describes this state says that

A Soul, Sometimes, After Having Achieved Great Heights of Right Belief,
Still Falls Back Into State of False Belief.
But Has Yet Not Fully Entered the Wrong Belief.
Such A Mid State Is Called Sasvadana.

—Smansuttam Sutra, 550

This *Sutra* throws a very important light on the fundamentals of the Shraman school of thought. It believes that progression of a soul from a lower state of being to a higher is not linear. It's not like a progression of a student from a lower class to a higher one, which if attained once cannot be reversed. On the contrary, this school of thought believes that a soul can fall back from a high point of existence to the lowest form of existence, depending upon his *Karmas* or actions.

However, since such a soul would have already had a glimpse of higher realms of spirituality, so he would not be at the same platform as the souls on the first stage who have yet to experience any further elevation. The past experiences of state of a higher platform will keep haunting him and he will not leave any stone unturned to relive it. There is a very famous Sufi song that captures this essence:

Firte hai kab se dar badar,
Aab is nagar aab us nagar,
Ik dusre ke hamsafar
Main aur meri aawargi
(and now I am wandering from here to there, from this city to that, together, me and my vagabonding)

Ham bhi kabhi aabad the,
Aise kahan barbad the,
Befiker the, aazad the,
Masrur the, dilshad the,
(I have also attained great heights once; I was not always a pauper like this. I had also seen great heights of no-worry and freedom and bliss and happiness)

Vo chaal aise chal gaya,
Ham bhuj gaye, dil jal gaya,
Nikle jala kar apna ghar,
Mein our meri aawargi
[and then he (the enemy?) played a great game, and I lost those heights, and I burnt my home (great castle of spiritual heights), all because of my vagabonding]

Wo Maah-e-vash Wo Maah-e-rooh
Wo Maah-e-kaamil Hu-ba-hu,
Theen Jis Ki Baatein Ku-ba-ku
Us Se Ajab Thi Guftaguu
Phir Yoon Huwa Wo Kho Gayi
Aur Mujh Ko Zid Si Ho Gai-
Laayeinge Us Ko Dhoond Kar
(Those great heights of ecstasy, those great days of freedom, when I was connected to myself. And then I lost all that. But then I also got adamant to rediscover it again.)

Jab Humdam-o-humraaz Tha
Tab Aur Hi Andaaz Tha
Aab sooz hai, tab saaz tha,
Aab sharma hai, tab naaz tha,
(When I was my own friend, then it was a totally different state of being. Now its only sorrow, then it was only happiness. Now I feel ashamed, then I felt pride.)

The above poem is no ordinary one. It has flown from the depths of the heart of someone who had experienced great bliss of spiritual heights and who has now lost it, but desires to regain the same.

This happens after the soul experiences a fall. Understanding it completely and being aware of it on the path to Godhood, is one of the most important steps on the path of upliftment of Soul.

On the spiritual ladder, the risk of falling back keeps rising in equal proportion as the progression of the soul. It's just like the progression of a mountaineer toward the summit. The more he keeps rising, the more dangerous it keeps getting. And this is a paradox. If a soul stays where it is, it will keep revolving in this universe. And, if it stops progressing higher on the spiritual ladder, there is every possibility that it will start falling down under. And if it keeps raising higher, then the risks of falling further also keeps rising in equal proportion.

It is perhaps for this reason that in India, and in the whole of East, there is great importance given to *Guru* or spiritual master for anyone who wants to elevate himself on the spiritual ladder. Since the master is someone who had either attained the topmost position, or is on a higher ladder than the disciple, He could be used as a mentor or guide on the spiritual path of the disciple.

The difference between the first state of soul and this second state of soul is important to be understood, as there would be a totally different approach of the two in further elevation.

The first soul is either totally ignorant of higher states of being possible for it or has deliberately kept itself in the dark about these states. Its progression to higher levels of existence will be very slow and full of hurdles.

The soul which has experienced this second level has already tasted the nectar of higher platforms possible for its existence. Its progression will be very fast. There is another Sufi poem that I would want to quote here:

Girta hua woh asma se
Aakar gira zameen par
Khwabon mein phir bhi badal hi the
Woh kehta raha magar
Allah ke bande hasde, jo bhi ho kal phir aayega
(And from the heights of the sky, he fell down to the Earth, but still he had the same clouds he ones travelled through in his thoughts. And he kept saying to himself—smile, Oh son of Great Allah! tomorrow will again be yours).

Kho ke aapne par hi to usne tha udnaa sikha
Gham ko aapne saath mein lele dard bhi tere kaam aayega
Allah ke bande hasde jo bhi ho kal phir aayega.
(You had attained those great heights by your own sheer will. Now take into account your mistakes, and that experience of mistakes will become a ladder for your future elevation. So, smile, Oh son of Great Allah! and pave the way for your own success.)

The above poem highlights the state of mind of someone who has experienced a fall from spiritual heights. He may have fallen back into the menial states of existence, but the desire to relive it still reins supreme. Such a person tells to himself that it was because of his own sheer willpower that he achieved those highs and all that he needs to do is to take account of the mistakes he made. This taking into account of one's mistakes and assuring the same are not repeated is the very essence of Shraman school of thought. We will discuss more over it as we proceed further.

3. *Misra-bhava* (State of Mixture of Right Belief and Wrong Belief)

This like the second stage we discussed above is also a very special state of being. As the soul or subtle mind moves out of *Mithyatva* for the first time in its *Atmic Cycle*, it does not arrive here, but elevates itself directly to the fourth stage of *Avirata Samyag Drishti* (State of Conscious Uncontrolled) that we will discuss ahead. But when such a soul, after having once achieved the fourth stage falls back in first state of *Mithyatva*, and then again moves ahead on spiritual elevation, then it arrives at this stage. We will discuss the logic behind this aberration during our discussion of the next stage.

The *Sutra* that goes into describing this state is as follows:

The Mixed State of Right Faith and Wrong Faith,
Which Can, in No Way be Split up Into Two.
It's Just like a Mixed Taste of Curd and Treacle (form of sugar)
Which can not be described as Sweet or Sour.
—Smansuttam Sutra, 551

A mixed state of affair! Where right belief and wrong belief co-exist! Where a soul can neither be described as living in *Mithyatva* nor be described as having transcended it. It's a state, where a person is totally engrossed in his material activities and thus looks similar to a person living in a state of wrong belief, but at the same time is also aware of higher realms of existence possible for him to achieve and thus can not be described as someone living in wrong belief. Just like a mixed taste of curd and sugar says Jina, which can neither be described as sweet, nor sour.

Discussion

- Jains say paying homage to anyone other than the Jina or Jain monks is *Mithyatva*. Is it correct to say so?
- What should we do to move out of the stage of *Mithyatva*?
- What are *Tatvas*?

Question

Jains say paying homage to anyone other then the Jina or the Jain monks is Mithyatva. Is it correct to say so?

The answer to this question would depend on the mindset of the person saying so. If he says these words because he is a Jain, and thus considers Jina alone as the enlightened master and his message alone as the true message, then this statement itself becomes a statement deeply drenched in *Mithyatva*.

We discussed above that *Mithyatva* in its *Abhigrahik* form is a state of mind with a faulty sight, which due to lack of knowledge and prejudiced by its bonds of love and passions, results in accepting his own philosophy as the sole truth and thus succumbs into accepting all its rituals, traditions, and rules without intellectually evaluating the logic and science behind them.

Thus, if this statement is being made by a Jain, just because he is a Jain without actually understanding the message of the Jina and having contemplated over it, then this statement is not correct.

But what if this is not the case. What if the person who is making this statement is a Jain scholar, and have fully understood the message of the Enlightened One?

In this case, what I feel is that such a person will never make this statement. Because if he has actually understood the Shraman Theology and have contemplated deeply on the knowledge of the *Nine Tatvas*, then he would know that any religion, and any master, irrespective of the fact that he belongs to the Jain tradition or not, if advocates their disciples to move ahead of their desires and passions is worthy of being paid homage.

And to the best of my understanding, every religion and every religious preacher of the world advocates the same. Their methodologies could be different. Their *modus operandi* could be different, but as long as they profess that people should leave the evil and perform good actions, they are perfectly in sync with the message of Jina and thus worthy of being paid homage.

The same even reflects in the greatest *Mantra* of Jain tradition—*The Namokar Mantra*. In this *Mantra*, as we discussed earlier too, the first homage is paid to the *Arihants*. *Arihants* are those souls, who have destroyed all those bondages of *Karma* (past actions) that keep a person tied to the world and forces it to be born again and again. It's worth noting that the *Arihants* are not just the Twenty-four great masters of Shraman tradition called *Tirthankars* of which Jina was the last, but all the souls who were able to break free. There are separate *Mantras* to pay homage to *Tirthankars*, but then they are next to *The Namokar Mantra*.

The second homage is paid to *The Siddhas*—The souls of those *Arihants* which have left their material bodies and are now in the state of *Nirvana*. Here also, no effort is being made to ensure that we pay homage to only those souls, who used the Jain tradition to achieve this high state, but every one of those, who achieved this state, irrespective of the path they choose.

The balance three homages are also completely secular in nature. These are paid to saints. From the head of their respective sects to the preachers to the monks. If they are saints, they deserve to be paid homage to, in spite of them being Jain or not.

Furthermore, the above statement that tends to convey that Jina alone is the truly enlightened master and Jain tradition alone the correct tradition also does not fit in tune with the Shraman principle of non-absolutism. Because as per this principle, the very statement that "this alone is right" is wrong!

Thus, as per my understanding considering paying homage to any one other than Jina and the Jain monks as *Mithyatva* is not in sync with this tradition. Jains alone do not have the exclusive rights to *Moksha* and that achieving it is the birth right of every individual.

Question
What should we do to move out of the stage of Mithyatva?

Jina says, "Not Having Complete Faith in *Tatva's* (elements) is *Mithyatva*." Thus the stepping stone out of *Mithyatva* is establishing faith in the *Tatvas*. It's a two-step process. At first, one acquires the knowledge of *Tatvas* and contemplates over them logically and analytically. The moment, a seeker does so, he steps out of *Mithyatva* and enters the Fourth *Guna* we will discuss in the next chapter.

Having analyzed the *Tatvas* and understood the logic behind them; the next step is to establish faith over them and starts using them for the betterment of ones own self. The moment a seeker does so, he further steps out of the Fourth *Guna* and enter the Fifth.

Thus, the key out of the stage of *Mithyatva* is the knowledge of *Tatvas*.

Question
What are Tatvas?

Tatvas is the deepest knowledge of Jain Theology. The entire Jain doctrine builds up around it.

To understand it, we first would need to reinitiate the fact that Shraman tradition does not believe in God who writes our destiny. Because if it was God who was deciding what we would get; then this world should have been in a state of a perfect Utopia. Then this world would have been a socialist place, where all would be equal with equal rights and equal access to all the resources.

But since this is not the case, thus it can well be interpreted that it's not the work of God. There is some one else, some other force that is playing a part in deciding as to who gets what. And that force is—us. We ourselves, as a result of our good and bad actions did that. We ourselves, through our virtuous and wicked deeds in past, wrote our destiny.

Tatvas is that master formula, which explains how we did it, and what's in store for us as a result of it. It is that master formula, which describes why we are—what we are. It explains why we do—that we do and what makes us do that. It explains why we get—that we get and why each one of us gets a different result for a similar action.

This formula breaks open—what determines our destiny. And the best part is that it also gives us the key to alter our destiny.

Now let's try and unravel the secret of this sacred knowledge. As a starting step, let's understand why we are—what we are; and why there is such a startling disparity in all of us.

We are all humans. It's because we have evolved into being a human after a long evolutionary process of our *Atmic Cycle*. Now if that alone was the case, then we all should have been more or less equal as we have passed through the same evolutionary process! If we analyze any other species, which as per Shraman Theology are on various phases of evolution, then we will not find much difference between them. Say, for example, all elephants are the same and live a similar life. There are no elephants that live like kings and no elephants that live like paupers. If it was just out of our evolutionary process, then this principle should have been applying on us too. But again this is not the case.

We are all different. The knowledge of *Tatvas* explain that it's because we all had performed a different set of actions in our past lives as humans or as animals or other lower forms in the evolutionary cycle, and thus we all our born with a different capital base of good and bad *Karmas* (actions). It is the result of this capital base of our good and bad *Karmas* that we are what we are.

If we are a king of a country or a president of a nation, then it's because our base of good actions in the past has outperformed the base of good actions of the ones we preside over. Similarly, if we are experiencing any physical, emotional or economic stresses, then it's been us who have reaped them for ourselves, by creating similar situations for others in the past.

Thus,to sum up, and to be able to enter into the knowledge of *Tatvas*, the first fundamental understanding is that what we are, is as a result of what we sowed for ourselves. And as a result of our past actions, we are carrying a burden of both good and bad actions in our kitty.

For the ease of understanding, let's name this kitty our *"Karmic Bank Account"* and draw a sketch as under (Fig. 2.1) to define our current state of being. This sketch will further help us understand how the various *Tatva's* determine our destiny in future. Let's place ourselves at the place of "myself" in Fig. 2.1 and understand that what so ever we are, is a result of our *"Karmic* account".

Now because we humans are a social animal, we are connected with other humans. These other humans, including ourselves, are referred to as *jeev* and are the first *Tatva*. These other *Jeev* could be our family, our friends, our associates or our rivals and enemies. These also include other humans with whom we do not have any connection but are a source of our admiration or hatred.

Thus, as we are, we share two types of relationships with other humans *(Jeev)*, viz. love and hate. These positive and negative relationships have been marked with a "+" and "–" signs in Fig. 2.1. This category of *Jeev*, apart from the humans, can also incorporate animals, insects and plants we live and deal with and our relationships with them.

Apart from the *Jeev* categories, we are also connected to certain material objects. These are material objects of our passions and desires and are referred to as *Ajeev* and are the second *Tatva*. These *Ajeev* are total of five in number, one among them being matter (called *Pudgal*) of which all the material objects we cherish are made off.

Since it's this matter *(Pudgal)* that directly affects us, thus for the moment we will just consider it alone and reserve the discussion on the balance four *Ajeev* substances for later discussion. This relationship with material objects can be in the form of attraction towards them (say for example desire to own a big house or car) and have been marked as "+" sign in Fig. 2.1. In some cases, this relationship can also be negative like abhorrence or disgust for material things which we do not feel are worthy of us and have been marked with "–" sign in Fig. 2.1.

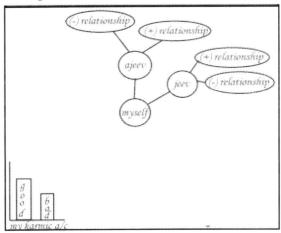

Now, here we are, as in the Fig. 2.1, connected with other living creatures and with some non-living objects and sharing a positive feeling of love and admiration and negative feelings of hate and envy.

What happens next? Based on our relationships we act. We start working for the betterment of those whom we love. And also start working against the ones we hate. Similarly, out of our infatuation or desire for the material objects, we also initiate actions, so as to acquire more of these objects and gratify our lust and desires.

This performance of actions, based on our love and hate relationships towards other beings and for the material objects is referred to as *Ashrav* or *Karmic* influx and is the third *Tatva*. These *Ashrav* (*Karmic* influx) then leads to *Karam-Bandh* (bondage of *Karmas*) which is referred to as the fourth *Tatva*.

This *Karam-Bandh* (bondage of *Karmas*) is of two subtypes. First of good actions that we perform called *Punya* and the second of bad actions that we perform called *Papa* and are respectively referred to as the fifth and the sixth *Tatvas*.

The *Papa* or bad actions we perform then further add on to our previously accumulated balance of bad actions in our *Karmic Bank Account* and the *Punya* or virtuous actions that we do add on to our previously accumulated balances of good actions. These good and bad actions then further end up determining our future course of being or our destiny.

All these additional *Tatvas* and the relationships they enjoy have been added to Fig. 2.2 for easy understanding.

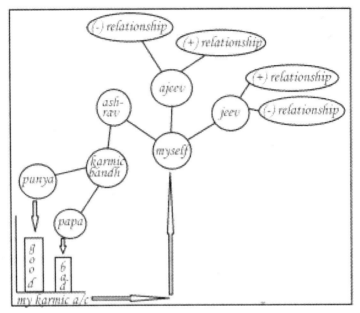

Fig. 2.2

And this is how the law of *Karmas* flow and determine our destiny.

These *Karmas* we accumulate, stick to our soul and wait to ripe and bear fruit at the appropriate time. The positive ones uplift us to better planes and shape for us a better future. The negative ones sink us to lower planes and result for us misfortunes, pains and anguish in future life.

The symbol of *Swastika* is a representation of this formula. One of its spokes represents our human life form and the balance three the three other forms of life our soul can experience, viz. the state of demigod referred to as *Dev-gati*, the state of animals (including insects and plants) called *Triyanch-gati* and the state of hellish being referred to as *Narak-gati*. Our accumulation of good and bad actions in our life form decides where we are born in the next.

If we end our life with a similar equation of good and bad

actions, as we were born with, we decide for ourselves a similar type of human life that we just lived. The greater we are able to accumulate the good actions, the better our destiny gets in future lives. If we take this graph of good actions so high that the good life we reaped for us is not possible to be experienced on this planet, then we are born on other planets or higher planes called heavens where living that type of life becomes possible (*Dev-gati*). And we continue to inhabit that plane, till those extra good *Karmas* are annihilated and thus we become capable of being born on our planet again.

Similarly, if it's the account of our bad *Karmas* that we ended up increasing for ourselves by the end of our life, then we write for ourselves, a life of far greater apathy and pain than the one we had just lived. In case this graph of bad deeds become so big that it's not possible to experience that degree of pain and anguish on our planet, we are born on other planets or planes called hell (*Narak-gati*), where we do that. And we continue to inhabit that plane till our bad *Karmas* gets annihilated and its graph comes back to a level, where we become capable if experiencing human form ones again.

Those among us, whose graph of bad *Karmas* goes so bust that even hells are not able to give them the pain they have sowed for themselves, then such persons end up destroying the senses they so painstakingly evolved and end up in forms with lesser sense organs than humans like those of insects and plants (*Trivanch-gati*). Such souls then start the process of evolution all over again, till they become capable of experiencing the human form once again.

And this cycle, represented by the four spokes of *Swastika* carries on and on, infinitely. It's already been an uncountable number of years we have been experiencing this repeated births and deaths in the above four forms of life which *Swastika* represents.

Now, there are a few illustrious souls, who are able to completely understand this formula and thus use it for their betterment. And to achieve it, they evaluate this complex relationship of *Tatvas* and the way they bind us—backwards.

Performing this backward analysis, they realize that the reason we experience the pains and pleasures is because of our *Karmic* account of good and bad actions. This Karmic accumulation is on account of the *Papa* (bad deeds) and the *Punya* (good deeds) that we perform. And the source of these *Karmic* accumulation or *Karam-Bandh* is the influx of *Karmas* or *Ashrav*.

Thus, as per this analysis, it can easily be pointed out that the *Ashrav*, is the gate, from where the entire process of *Karam-Bandh* starts. It's this point that needs to be worked at, and the rest will follow on its own accord. Thus, these illustrious ones start mending this place! They become aware of their actions, and ensure that they minimize the acts which result in miseries for them in future and maximize the acts, which they could bank on in future.

It's simple arithmetics. Just as in accounts, assets = capital + liability, same way, our assets base of *Karmic* bank account is equal to the capital of good *Karmas* we acquire plus the liabilities we raise for ourselves by performing bad *Karmas*. Any person, who has even the slightest knowledge of basic accounting, knows the fact that maximization of capital and minimization of liabilities is the key to success in material life. The illustrious ones start practising the same formula in the spiritual life too.

Another very important revelation the above understanding of *Tatvas* we discussed so far makes, is fixing the responsibility of our actions. Normally, a feeling pervades in general that "man is nothing, but a puppet in the hands of God." Shraman Theology completely rubbishes this claim. It says such words are just a façade to escape responsibility. It entirely fixes the responsibility of our actions on us. We do, what we do, not because there is a God playing with us or directing our actions, but we do, what we do because of our own desires, lust, passions and greed.

The knowledge of *Tatvas* is the source of this claim. If we evaluate the above graph, a bit minutely, we can easily conclude the same.

The graph clearly points the reason of our performance of actions (*Ashrav*) towards us. It's us, who are doing these actions. And thus it's us who are responsible and need to take accountability, rather than pointing fingers on any one else.

This above understanding is the crux of knowledge of *Tatvas* as it gives the key to write our destiny to us. Because if it's us who are responsible for the actions we do, then we can ensure that we perform only those actions that lead to a better future for us and fordo the one's that can lead to pain and anguish. Thus, we can decide our own future! We can plan for ourselves, what ever we wish. Pain or pleasure, misery or bliss! It's all in our own hands.

This is a point of great realization. The moment a seeker fully understands this basic principle, he starts mending his actions and immediately raises himself to the fifth *Guna* (spiritual stage). But that's not all the knowledge of *Tatvas* have to offer us. There are still greater depths to unravel and more treasures, far more precious to be discovered.

Using the above formula, we can ensure that we create for ourselves better lives in future and escape the miseries of pain and anguish. But what happens next? Say for example, we created for ourselves the place of king of demigods—The *Indra,* in the highest of heavens that exist. Now what happens? We live that life, but only as long as the good things we did get exhausted, and once they do, we get back to our human form, back in the pain and anguish of this world! Back to our home—on Earth.

To explain this further, masters use the following example. They say consider a person who performed great hard work and earned for himself huge wealth. Now he leaves his native village and travels the world. He lives in the best of hotels and relishes the best of the pleasures this world has to offer. Now a point comes when he ends up exhausting all his hard earned money, and thus comes back to his native village and starts all over.

Same says the masters, is the case for the life's we relish in heavens. It's just an after-effect of the good deeds we have accumulated for ourselves and are not eternal. They are just like a holiday, and not a permanent residence.

Now this is not a very pleasing picture. If all the good work that we do can just result for us a short holiday, and after having received its due, we get back to the square one—the place we started from, then certainly, heavens are not a very worthy place to achieve! They may be the best place amid all the four types of life forms we live in, but still not a permanent reprieve from the cycle of transmigration of soul.

This understanding sets the background for further analysis of the formula of *Tatvas*. The seekers among us, who realize the above, go into further contemplation of the *Tatvas*. Having realized the futility of actions, both good and bad, they start exploring the possibility of moving beyond actions. If it's our actions that lead us to better or bad places, and if these better and bad places then lead us back to this material world, to perform more actions, then performance of actions—The *Ashrav* becomes the axis because of which we revolve in various life forms. Good or bad, heavens or hells, or a heaven-like life or hell-like life here on our own planet. It's the axis of *Ashrav*, which results in all this.

This leads them to asking themselves a question. They ask themselves—after all why do we do actions at the first place? What is it that leads us into actions? And a deep psychoanalysis starts.

The formula of *Tatvas* has the answer. The figure 2.2 has the clue. If we analyze this figure keenly, we will realize that actions initiate because of our positive and negative relationships towards the *Jeev* (living) and *Ajeev* (material objects).

Thus it's these relationships that are the main culprit and make us perform actions and lead to *Ashrav* (*Karmic* influx). These positive relationships of love and admiration are called *Raga* and the negative feelings of hate and envy are called *Dwesha* and are the root cause of our binding ourselves to this never-ending cycle of transmigration of soul.

Having thus identified the root cause of the source of *Karmas*, the blessed ones among us put an end to these relationships, and renounce the world and become monks and nuns. As a result of this renunciation, they uproot the entire process of influx of *Karmas* and increase of our karmic burden—our *Karmic* asset base. And as soon as this influx of *Karmas* stops, what occurs is—*Samvar*. It's the seventh *Tatva* and is opposite of *Ashrav*. *Ashrav* was the influx of *Karmas* which resulted in increase of our *Karmic* bank account by acquiring more capital (*Punya*) and liabilities (*papa*). The *Samvar* is the stoppage of further addition of *Karmas* to this account.

This is the state of great achievement. The moment a seeker succeed in achieving this state, he uplifts himself to the sixth *Guna* that we will discuss in detail later in this discussion.

But unfortunately, just performing *Samvar* is not sufficient to break free from this cycle of transmigration of soul. The huge mountain of *Karmic* bondages that we had accumulated for ourselves in our *Karmic* bank account still looms large over us. These good and bad actions which we have been accumulating all our life and all the previous lives we have lived so far till we entered *Samvar* are still balance in our account. They still need to be paid back.

Stages of Mithyatva—The Legacy of Our Animalistic Past

Now, as these past *Karmic* bondages still waiting to ripe, fructifies and come back to haunt the seeker, it opens two possibilities for him. The first is that as a result of their effect, he responds back. Doing that would mean performing another action and thus *Ashrav* or an influx of more karma's. This influx of *Karmas* will then lead to *Karmic* bondage and addition of a bad or a good deed back into our *Karmic* bank account. The second option is to accept the fructified *Karma* as is and face it—head on. This will lead to annihilation of that *Karma* and thus a reduction in burden of our *Karmic* debt.

This facing and annihilating the *Karma* is called *Nirjara* and is the eighth *Tatva*. A seeker that is able to perform *Nirjara* accepts all that happens to him, willingly and without any reaction on his part. This was perhaps the reason Buddha did not react, when someone spitted on His face. This was perhaps the reason that Jesus did not react, while being crucified. This was the reason why Jina did not react, while some one nailed His ears.

And as the seeker keep performing *Nirjara*, the *Karmic* bank account of good and bad deeds that he had accumulated for himself over time starts annihilating. And the moment they annihilate completely, opens the ninth *Tatva*—The *Moksha*. The seeker gets liberated. He escapes the transmigration of soul that the four spokes of *Swastika* represents. The soul now rises above heavens and hells and the humans and the animals and insects and plants and become a *Siddha*—A God. It's now represented by drawing a semi-circle with a star on top—above the symbol of *Swastika*. This semi-circle and star are the same as the symbol of moon and star in Islam. Only difference is that the semicircular moon above *Swastika* is not tilted. It rests straight. This is the symbol of Godhood, of *Siddha*—The God in Shraman tradition. Besides this moon and star, three dots are placed below it and above the four spokes of *Swastika*. The knowledge of *Tatvas* we are discussing here is one of these dots. We will discuss the balance two later in another volume of this book. Together, they complete the *Swastika*.

These three last *Tatvas* we just discussed, when come into play, are indicated as under in the Fig. 2.3.

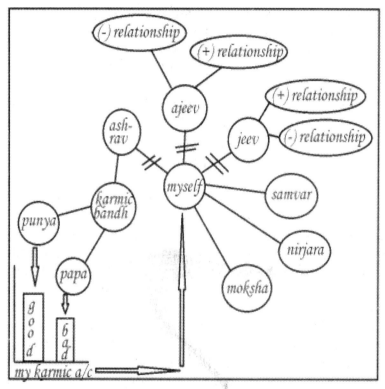

Fig. 2.3

These nine put together, viz. *Jeev* (soul of living beings), *Ajeev* (material objects), *Ashrav* (influx of *Karmas*), *Karmic-Bandh* (bondages of *Karmas*), *Punya* (virtuous deeds), *Papa* (vicious deeds), *Samvar* (stoppage of new *Karmas*), *Nirjara* (annihilation of past *Karmas*) and *Moksha* (liberation from past *Karmas*) are the *Nine Tatvas*.

Understanding this relationship and contemplating it analytically and logically is the key to break free from *Mithyatva*.

Arrival of Samkit—The Blossoming of Humanity

4

Arrival of Samkit—The Blossoming of Humanity

He Is Not Able to Detach Himself from Desires of Sense Organs and from Hurting of the Movable or Immovable Beings for His own Self Interests. But Still Contemplates Deeply (Shradhan) Over the Tatva's (elements) As Proclaimed by the Enlightened Masters.
—*Samansuttam Sutra*, 552

SAMKIT IS SUPPOSED to be the greatest virtue of a human. With the knowledge of *Tatvas*, the process of arrival of *Samkit* starts. And the starting point of this virtue is the fourth *Guna*.

4. Avirata Samyag Drishti (State of Conscious Uncontrolled)
This is the most important stage in the evolution of soul or subtle mind in its *Atmic Cycle*. It is at this stage that a soul takes its first most important step to its further elevation to Godhood. Here for the first time, it steps out of its animalistic instincts and starts its journey upwards. It's at this point that the soul actually attains humanity in the true sense of the word.

In the *Atmic Cycle* of a soul, this state comes just after *Mithyatva* the first time during its spiritual elevation, so it can be called as a—Gateway to Godhood.

It is at this stage that a person becomes aware of higher realms of existence possible for him to achieve. When Jina refers to His earlier births, the first story He tells is of the incarnation when He was told the path to enlightenment. He was then a forester who used to gather wood for construction work in the kings palace. One day He found some wandering monks lost in the jungle. He offered His food to them and escorted them out of the woods. As the monks took leave, in return they imparted Him the knowledge of the path to Godhood.

This was the point when His soul entered this state of *Avirata Samyag Drishti*. This knowledge then changed the course of His life and paved His way to enlightenment. The above incident took place on a planet different from our Earth and in a parallel universe than what we see out there in space. We will discuss about all these parallel universes and planets that support human life forms in later volumes of this book.

During our discussion of the third stage, a logical understanding of why a soul enters this fourth stage straight out of *Mithyatva* the first time during its elevation in its *Atmic Cycle* was postponed. The logic is that the third stage is a mixture of someone totally engrossed in the material world and yet aware of the higher realms of existence possible for him. A soul, which for the first time is moving out of *Mithyatva* in its *Atmic Cycle*, becomes aware of it only when it's told of these possibilities. And as soon as a soul gets acquainted of this knowledge, it immediately uplifts itself to this fourth stage of *Avirata Samyag Drishti* bypassing the third. So this stage, the first time during its elevation to higher *Gunas* comes directly after the first. But when such a soul falls back to *Mithyatva* and starts its journey back upwards, since it already is aware of the possibilities of higher planes of existence possible, may enters third after first and then gradually elevates itself to this fourth stage.

The *Sutra* that describes this state says:

He Is Not Able to Detach Himself from Desires of Sense Organs and from Hurting of the Movable or Immovable Beings for His own Self Interests. But Still Contemplates Deeply (Shradhan) Over the Tatva's (elements) As Proclaimed by the Enlightened Masters.
—Samansuttam Sutra, 552

We discussed *Tatvas* in the last section. Those among us, who would enter into contemplation on the same, would find themselves having uplifted to this *Guna*. This is because contemplation of *Tatvas* enables us to attain the right vision. It then helps the seeker to discover for himself, the actions which are worthy of being carried out and the actions which are futile.

But, in spite of that, the seeker at this stage is not able to renounce all that is bad, and inculcate all that is good.

A person at this state of mind contemplates that all desires are useless. He knows well that fulfilling one immediately leads to the rise of another and the process carries on, and the desire to desire never gets fulfilled. But this vision fails to reflect in his attitude towards life.

A person in this state of mind realizes that anger is bad, and tries to control it, but fails whenever an opportunity to get angry arises. Such a person knows that desire for sensual pleasures is a type of disease and contemplates on how to overcome it, but fails whenever an opportunity to fulfill this abstinence arises.

Why does it happen? This issue was discussed at one of the knowledge sessions of The Art of Living organization. The discussion does throw a very deep insight on discovering the reason of this basic failure of humans to transform their experiences into actions.

It was tried to be explained using two words. These two words are *Anubhava* and *Anubhuti*. *Anubhava* means an experience. It is an after-effect on us because of an outward situation and is totally dependent on that situation. The experience will last only till that outward situation exists and will cease to exist as soon as that outward situation changes. On the contrary, *Anubhuti* is a state of a deep insight. When experience becomes deep enough and gets rooted deep in our psyche, it becomes *Anubhuti* or Insight. Now it is no more dependent on outward experience. Rather, now it becomes a part of our being.

If this Insight or *Anubhuti* is that something gives us pleasure and bliss, then our nervous system automatically starts taking interest in it, and if our Insight or *Anubhuti* towards a particular action is that it gives us pain and frustration, then our nervous system automatically negates all those actions. Whenever situations of repeating those actions arise, by default, our nervous system takes a negative attitude towards that particular action and makes us aware of not repeating it.

Achieving such a state is a moment of great achievement and will occur to us gradually on our path to Godhood. *Shraman* theology calls it the process of *Samyag Darshan* (Right Insight) leading to *Samyag Chariter* (Right Character). We will discuss more on that later as we get deeper into the *Sutras* of the Shraman school of thought, but for the moment, for a seeker at this fourth basic stage of spiritual growth, this is still utopia.

As of now, the seeker is too deeply entrenched in his vices to make this transformation happen. Perhaps the experiences of such a person are still not as deep enough as the roots of his desires and passions. The vision of Right Faith has dawned upon him and is visible as well, but only when the darkness of passions and desires are not in existence. When the darkness of desires and passions are in their full flow, the vision of right faith fades away in front of the all-pervasive darkness of these vices.

It's just like stars disappear when the sky gets cloudy. They still exist, but because of presence of clouds, they become non-existent. Similar are these visions of right faith, which spark into existence at the fourth stage, but are still not bright enough, to be visible when the dark clouds of passions and desires are at their full bloom!

A person at this fourth ladder of spiritual rise has still not achieved such a state of mind that his *Anubhava* could become *Anubhuti* and thus result in his staying away from actions that are bound to result in pain and frustration for him.

Another thing that the *Sutra* says about a person at this stage is that he does not stop hurting the movable or immovable creatures for his own self-interest, even though he has fully understood the message of the enlightened masters. What does this mean?

The Shraman school of thought divides this world into two types of beings. One it calls *Sthavar Jeev* which means immovable beings like plants and second is called *Tras Jeev* which means beings that can move like animals, insects and us humans. The Shraman school has always believed that both these types of beings are living creatures and manifestations of the same soul and all of them command the same basic fundamental right to exist. As a human, someone on the top of the ladder of evolution, we do not have any right to kill or uproot any other form of being, on a similar or lower level of existence. This message has been consistent in teachings of all the Great Masters of the Shraman school of thought including Buddha.

A person at this fourth stage is aware of this message, but has still not started practising it in his day-to-day life. He does not mind killing beings at a lower platform than his own for his self-interest.

Let's try and get a bit deeper into this thesis of Shraman Theology of respecting lower forms of being. Understanding the depth and logic behind this basic fundamental tenet will help us further deeply understand the true meaning of the *Sutras* we will discuss ahead.

We humans have always believed that everything in this world exists to be used by us. Be it vegetation or animals. They have been created by nature—for us. Just as animals feed on plants, stronger animals feed on less strong animals similarly; in this food chain, we humans have a right and authority to consume every lower form of being than ours. This is the fundamental concept behind non-vegetarianism and of course, the logic looks very apt.

But then let's explore this logic a bit deeper. If animals have a right to feed on plants, if stronger animals have a right to feed on feeble animals, and if humans have a right to feed on animals, then applying this logic, can it be said that the stronger of us humans have a right to feed on the feeble humans? Then is it right for humans to feed on humans too? Then is it right to kill, and suppress, and exploit one human by another?

We humans have actually been doing this in the past. The race of humans that made themselves a bit better and more civilized in the modern sense of the word, has been doing this on other human races who preferred to live in greater harmony with nature. Ancient Cretes were supposed to do it. They fed themselves on humans. They demanded human sacrifices from Athenians. Minotaur was a personification of this Crete high headedness.

Slavery was another expression of this thought process, where some of us humans thought that it was ok to treat other humans like animals and buy and sell them and suppress them and torture them for self-interest. Similarly, there are many other examples in human history. There have been numerous madmen, who thought that they are the best humans, and thus have a fundamental right to dictate and rule over other humans and use and abuse them for their own self-interest. Hitler, Napoleon, Alexander,

Changez Khan and many more! The list is endless. The above are just some of these madmen who made to the top of this list.

If there is someone who did not like the above comparison between Alexander and Chengez Khan, then he should read about his atrocities during his expedition of North-Western India which is today's Pakistan.

Fortunately, humanity today has moved beyond that ugly past. Human values are greatly respected across the globe. But we are yet to develop the same compassionate heart for other forms of life. We still do not mind using and abusing animals for our own selfish interest. We still feel that since they are inferior to us, they do not have any feelings or rights, and we can do whatever we want to them.

How correct is it? Let's try and find an answer to this question from another dimension.

I remember seeing a movie during my childhood. The movie was *Super Man*. The hero of the movie was a man from another planet, where life had prospered and evolved at a higher pace than our planet, and therefore he was bestowed with powers much higher than us humans on Earth. The villains in the movie were a group of three super humans from the same planet as Super Man who wanted to enslave earthlings and develop this planet as per their whims.

Super Man tried to resist their efforts and fought for the sake of humans. This surprised the villains, and one of them asked the other in their vicious group the reason why Super Man took so much care of the earthlings.

"Perhaps like pets", replied the other.

In the eyes of those super human villains, the status of us earthlings was no more than the status of animals in the eyes of us humans. And they were correct in their own right. They were on a higher platform of evolution than us humans. Just as we humans do not mind abusing animals for our own self-interest, similarly, those super humans, did not see anything wrong in abusing us. But then they were seen as villains in the eyes of humans.

Perhaps, this is the status that humans have in the eyes of animals. It has been scientifically proven that they also live in their societies, support their own families and care and love each other. They have their own way of life. But we humans disrupt it all by forcing ourselves over them. The movie of super human hero and villains was a work of fiction. But what we do to animals on a daily basis is factual. Like the super humans in the movie, we are at a higher platform of existence than our animal counterparts.

And just as in the movie, we humans did not like anyone more powerful than us trying to overpower us and use or abuse us for their own plans for this creation, similarly, animals feel when we take away their basic right to exist and live the way they want to live by forcing ourselves over them.

The Shraman school advocated that just as we humans demand a right to exist, so do animals. Just as we humans feel sad when anyone of our loved one gets killed, so do animals. This very thought is the genesis of the philosophy of *Ahimsa*—The Theory of Live and Let Live.

A seeker at this fourth ladder of spiritual existence is not able to realize this basic philosophy of right to existence for all the beings—be it animals or plants. He has evolved higher than his counterparts like Hitler and Chengez Khan, and has started respecting basic human rights of his fellow human beings. But he still has not developed a soft corner for other forms of beings in this vast creation. He still does not mind to do on animals, what the tyrants like above did to humanity. From Shraman Theology's point of view, there is little difference between our butcher houses and Hitler's concentration camps. Nature gets slaughtered in both the cases.

Arrival of Samkit—The Blossoming of Humanity

Discussion

- Is killing animals as bad as killing humans? Is comparing butcher houses to Hitler's concentration camps a right comparison?
- If non-vegetarianism is bad as it results in killing, is it ok to eat meat where we did not initiate killing ourselves?
- The structure of the world is such that we cannot escape killing. From simple acts like walking, talking and even breathing, there are beings that are constantly being killed. Doing other activities required in our daily routines lead to far more deaths. Is it not absurd to make such a hue and cry for the death of one single being killed to feed a human and totally ignore the numerous others whom we keep killing on daily basis?

Question

Is killing animals as bad as killing humans? Is comparing butcher houses to Hitler's concentration camps a right comparison?

The question arises out of a belief that we humans and animals are not equal, and thus a comparison between them is not a proper one. And this belief arises from the feeling that we are a better, more evolved race or life form, and thus are superior to them.

This belief is true because we have a better set of senses than our animal counterparts. Thus, killing humans is a greater sin than killing animals. Now the question arises that is the comparison between our butcher houses and Hitler's concentration camps justified?

Let's try and explore this comparison.

Because of our better set of senses, we humans have made ourselves the masters of this planet and have thrown all its resources at our disposal. Thus, we feel that this entire world, including other forms of life, exist for our use. This is the reason we do not associate with them. This is the reason we do not find anything wrong to what we do to the forms of life lower than ours. As long as it's serving our purpose, giving us better health, and giving us a better form of life, we approve it. This is the reason we do not find anything wrong in our butcher houses. Because for us, the lesser forms of life, just exist to be used and abused for our own betterment.

Now following the same logic, let's look at the concentration camps. These were the butcher houses set by the Nazis, to kill humans. Those humans whom the Nazis felt were an inferior lot, and thus did not fit into their plans for their land.

These fanatics Nazis considered themselves as Aryans, descendents of some demigods from the outer world, and thus a race superior to the rest of the humanity! Thus, in their own accord, they were somewhat similar to the aliens in the movie *Super Man* that we discussed above. Some one over and above the rest of humanity that inhabits this world, and unnecessarily consumes its resources.

So, in their own right, in order to create a better place, worthy of living for themselves, they attempted to start cleaning their land of whom they considered non-important, and in this process created the concentration camps.

Now spot the similarity between the two. Butcher houses are a place where we annihilate the lesser forms of life because we do not consider them worthy of being granted right to live. Concentration camps were a place where the Nazis did the same for the forms of life they considered unworthy. For them the Jews they killed were worth nothing more than the animals we kill in our butcher houses. There is a clear-cut high headedness in both the cases. And it's this high headedness that is the culprit.

And this is where the similarity lies between our butcher

Arrival of Samkit—The Blossoming of Humanity

houses and the Hitler's concentration camps. The high headedness and resulting absence of compassion! The absence of sympathy and regard towards the ones over whom we preside! It's this lack of kindness that makes us blind towards the fact that those whom we kill had a right to live their own way of life! It is this lack of consideration that makes us deaf to their screams demanding equality. Nature gets slaughtered in both cases. Humanity gets shamed at both places.

Question
If non-vegetarianism is bad as it results in killing, is it ok to eat meat where we did not initiate killing ourselves?

One of the basic fundamentals of economics is that demand leads to supply. If there is no demand, supply dries up automatically. So let's be clear that if we are non-vegetarian, then the entire killing that takes place on our planet is being done to feed us. Because the ones who do so, know that there is demand and that their product will sell. This is the reason they keep their stocks ready.

So it's faulty to consider that we did not initiate killing, and thus are not responsible for the death of the animal we are feeding on. On the contrary, if we are non-vegetarian, then we are responsible for killing of every animal that gets butchered because it was killed in order to feed us. Weather we ended up consuming it or not do not make any difference.

Question
The structure of the world is such that we cannot escape killing. From simple acts like walking, talking and even breathing, there are beings that are constantly being killed. Doing other activities required in our daily routines lead to far more deaths. Is it not absurd to

make such a hue and cry for the death of one single being killed to feed a human and totally ignore the numerous others whom we keep killing on daily basis?

It's true that the structure of our world is based on the very foundations of violence. We do in our day-to-day life and in our normal daily routine end up killing a lot of creatures. The question is then why do we create such a hue and cry for death of the ones we kill to quench our hunger.

The answer perhaps lies in the question itself. The killing or the violence that takes place on account of our activities happens. We do not do them intentionally. We do not act to kill anyone. We are on our way. We are just performing our daily activities. And if in this process, an insect, or any other living creature does get annihilated, then it's not being done for the purpose to take away its life. It just happened!

But when we kill someone for our food, we do that intentionally. Its purpose is to take away life of that creature purposefully. When a butcher kills an animal, he does that to sell off its meat. When a consumer buys that meat, he does that to quench his desires of senses, the lust of tongue.

And that's what makes the two cases different. The intention! Jina valued this intention greatly. For Him, our intention behind doing an activity was more important than the activity itself. As per Shraman school: *intention to kill is an act of violence* (Himsa), *and intention not to kill is non-violence* (Ahimsa). *This is irrespective of the fact that a being actually gets killed or not.*

Thus, killing or not killing is not important. It's the intention of the doer that is. If we tried to kill some one, but that person escaped, still at heart, the violence is done. Similarly, if we did not intend to kill some one, but death of a being occurred, still at heart, it is not considered violence.

And this perhaps gives the answer as to why multiple

unintended deaths of living creatures that are caused by our daily actions are not considered worthy of raising any hue and cry, and why even a single intended death of a living creature considered such an unworthy act.

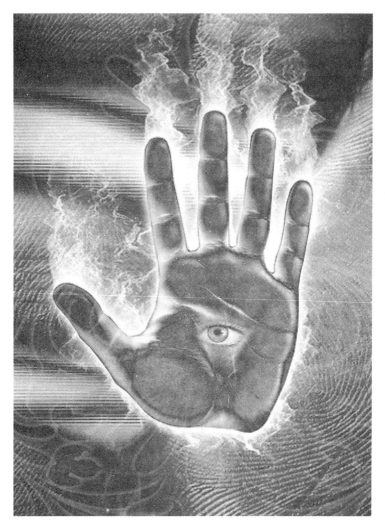

Stepping into Desh Virakt—Declaration of Freedom

5

Stepping into Desh Virakt—Declaration of Freedom

One Who Desists From Killing of Mobile Living Beings, But Not From the Immobile Ones Like Vegetation, And Yet Who Has Unwavering Faith (Shradha) in the Enlightened Ones.
—*Samansuttam Sutra*, 553

AT THE FOURTH *Guna* (stage), *Samkit* (right vision of living a life) arrives. Gradually, it starts flowering and spreading its fragrance and takes the seeker out of the fourth and stations him at the fifth *Guna*.

5. *Desh Virakt (State of Defining One's boundaries)*
This is the beginning of claiming one's control over oneself. Declaration of freedom, by oneself, from oneself, and for oneself! This is the announcement of liberation from ones own mind. From one's own desires. From one's own passions.

In this state, man says, enough is enough, and rebels against his own untamed mind of desires and passions and decides his own course of actions. He now decides his own Dos and Don'ts.

This needs to be understood in comparison to the fourth stage. At the fourth, man receives the right vision, but fails to put that into action. Here, at this fifth stage, his vision starts reflecting in his actions. Until the fourth stage, his vision towards life has changed, but his way of life remains unchanged. In this fifth stage, his vision towards life, changes the very course and direction of his life.

He decides that he will no longer permit himself to be carried over by his desires, and decides a course of action for himself. He gives himself a direction. And thus this stage is called—*Desh Virakt*—i.e. defining one's boundaries. Now, he starts consciously controlling all his actions. Or in other words, he gains control over his conscious mind.

This is one of the most important stages in the progression of a seeker towards enlightenment. It symbolizes the declaration of one's own freedom and mastery over one's own desires and passions. That's why most of the enlightened masters of India including Buddha and Shankar had called their disciples—*Swami* which means Master, i.e. masters of their mind. The source of the *Sutras* under review, The Jina Himself was called *Mahavira Swami* in His times. *Swami* is a person, who takes control of his life in his own hands, and refuses to be a slave to his desires and passions.

The importance of this state can be better understood by taking an example of a river. Just as a river can reach the ocean only if it flows within specified boundaries; or otherwise it gets lost in wilderness, similar is the condition of a seeker. To elevate one's self, it is important that a seeker sets boundaries for itself and cuts short all useless outflows of its energies so as to direct them all towards one direction—towards Godhood.[1]

The *Sutra*, on this stage of a seeker, says:

One Who Desists From Killing of Mobile Living Beings, But Not From the Immobile Ones Like Vegetation, And Yet Who Has Unwavering Faith (Shradha) in the Enlightened Ones.
—*Samansuttam Sutra,* 553

This *Sutra* throws a very important light on the actions of seeker who has reached this stage. It says the seeker at this stage turns vegetarian.

As discussed earlier, this school of thought believes that killing of all forms of life is bad. Be it mobile beings (*Tras Jeev*) like animals and insects or immobile beings (*Sthavar Jeev*) like vegetation. This school believes that all forms of life are manifestation of the same life force that makes our existence possible. Thus, killing any form of life is actually killing or hurting our very own life force.

At this stage, a seeker has reached towards realizing this basic fundamental and thus abstains himself from any action of violence towards mobile living beings. He is still not in a state to rise above hurting the immobile ones like vegetation, but still has rooted himself deep enough in spirituality, to make his further progression possible.

However, it should be remembered that vegetarianism is more of a state of mind. We will discuss more about it as we proceed. But I refer to it here so as to highlight that all those who are vegetarians by birth, i.e. not eating meat because the family they are born does not consider it virtuous, should not misjudge themselves to be at this stage by the virtue of their birth itself! They may be vegetarian, not because they have achieved an insight that killing is bad. On the contrary, they may be vegetarians just because they have been conditioned into accepting that eating meat is bad, but without any real love or respect for fellow living creatures in their hearts.

A seeker rises to this state only out of love and compassion for the forms of being that are lower to him in the cycle of evolution and abstains from harming them to quench his desires. It is only when a seeker has achieved such a kind heart; he becomes vegetarian in the true sense of the word.

Before we proceed further, there is another dimension of this *Sutra* that needs to be contemplated. The *Sutra* says that at this stage, a seeker "desists from killing of mobile living beings, but not from the immobile ones like vegetation".

Why does this *Sutra* specifically says that a seeker does not desist from killing immobile living creatures like vegetation? Does this mean that just as a seeker has come to a state of awareness where he has realized that killing of animals for the sake of one's food is not a noble act, similarly in future he would also come to a stage, where he would realize that killing of vegetation is also not a sensible thing?

Perhaps yes!

As the seeker will continue his further elevation up the ladder to Godhood, he would come to a state of being where he would get more and more sensitive of the effect of his actions on nature. In this process, he will come to a state of mind where he would start questioning his actions and would like to take the least possible from nature to survive. At the current stage, he becomes highly conscious that his actions do not cause pain and death to any mobile living creature. Gradually, he develops the same kindheart towards vegetation too. There is a beautiful story in Jain scriptures that explain this phenomenon. The story states as follows:

There Were Six Travelers. They Had Lost Their Way in a Dense Forest. They Were Extremely Hungry. After Some Time They Saw a Tree Full of Ripe Fruits. They Thought of Eating Those Fruits and Started Contemplating of What They Should do. The First Thought of Uprooting the Whole Tree and Eating its Fruits. The Second Thought of Cutting off the Tree From Trunk and Eating Over its Fruits. The Third Thought of Chopping off One of its Main Branch and Eating its Fruits. The Fourth Thought of Chopping off Side Branches to Eat its Fruits. The Fifth Thought of Plucking and Consuming the Required Number of Fruits Only. The Sixth Thought That Only the Fruits That Fall Naturally off the Tree Should be Consumed.
—Samansuttam Sutra, 537–38

All the six travellers in this story are contemplating about eating vegetation. But there is a huge difference in their level of sensitivity towards nature. The first among them is least bothered about the effect of his actions. He does not mind killing the whole tree to quench his hunger. The second traveller is also least bothered about the effect of his actions. The third, fourth and fifth travellers keep getting more and more prudent of their actions and the effect it will have on the tree. The last traveller is perhaps the most sensitive of all as he thinks that even plucking of fruits will hurt the tree and so prefers to wait for fruits to fall off by themselves.

Stepping into Desh Virakt—Declaration of Freedom 87

This is what the *Sutra* means when it says "desists from killing of mobile living beings, but not from the immobile ones like vegetation". The first two of the above six travellers are perhaps on this ladder and the rest are more and more sensible.

The seeker as he grows further on the path to Godhood, slowly, comes to a realization that his actions should not cause pain to any form of life, be it mobile or immobile, so, as a first step, he turns vegetarian and then gradually also gets choosier about the type of vegetation he consumes. Some Jain monks do not eat the vegetation from the roots of plants. The logic perhaps is that when the roots are plucked over to take out that vegetation, it leads to death of that plant. So this equates such vegetation to meat. Or, in other words, just as eating meat is not a righteous act as it results in the death of a living creature; similarly eating roots of a plant is also not gracious as it also results in death of a living creature.

Let's remember that this is not the case as yet of the seeker at the fifth stage. I am just trying to give you a glimpse of what lies ahead and the depth of the Shraman ideology.

Discussion

- The only difference in the fourth and the fifth stages seems to be a shift from non-vegetarianism to vegetarianism. Is this correct understanding?
- Is it absolutely important to turn vegetarian to move ahead on the path to Godhood?
- What about Buddhist? They are Shraman, and constitute its biggest branch. They are mostly non-vegetarian? Are they all flawed?

Question
The only difference in the fourth and the fifth stages seems to be a shift from non-vegetarianism to vegetarianism. Is this correct understanding?

As per my understanding, the above statement is not correct.

Turning vegetarian is not the difference between the fourth and the fifth stages. It's a result of the difference that occurs in the mindset of the seeker as he enters the fifth. Turning vegetarian is just a reflection, a shadow of his raised awareness.

The main difference between the two stages is in the change in mindset of the seeker. With acquiring the knowledge of *Tatvas* a right vision to lead the life gets planted at the fourth. Here at this stage, it sprouts. The *Samkit* now starts taking roots.

At the fourth stage, the seeker starts questioning his actions. He evaluates his actions based on the knowledge of *Tatvas*. Knowing the fact that his actions will bounce back on him and will be shaping his destiny, he asks himself if the action he is performing is worth the cost of that action. Here at the fifth, he starts plugging those actions which he feels are not worth the cost.

Turning vegetarian is one of those actions. As the seeker rises above the fourth *Guna*, and immerses deeper into the spirituality, he starts experiencing the same compassion towards animals as he felt for the rest of the humanity at the fourth stage.

Jina says:

> *Just As You Do Not Want To Be Subjugated To Pain,*
> *So Does The Balance Of Living Creatures.*
> *Thus Knowing This Principle, Respect The Right Of Others To Live*
> *With Complete Dignity And Carefulness.*
> —*Samansuttam Sutra,* 150

Having realized the fact that killing someone, or becoming a cause of someone's death, who at the time of being slaughtered would have experienced the same pain and anguish as he himself would do, puts an end to this action and as a result, turns vegetarian.

Thus, turning vegetarian is a reflection of another higher virtue—Compassion.

Stepping into Desh Virakt—Declaration of Freedom

Question
Is it absolutely important to turn vegetarian to move ahead on the path to Godhood?

Whenever the term that something is absolute comes, in my understanding, the answer as per Shraman Theology should be no. It's just my personal opinion. But yes, it certainly is the greatest virtue a seeker acquires on the path to Godhood.
Explaining the importance of this virtue, Jina says:

> *Just As There Is No Mountain Higher Than Mt Meru,*
> *Just As There Is Nothing More Extensive Than Sky,*
> *Similarly There Is Nothing That is Equal To The Principle Of Ahimsa (theory of live and let live)*
> —*Samansuttam Sutra,* 158

Thus, Jina says that it's the greatest single virtue. The single greatest act that a human is capable of performing—granting others the right to live, the same way as we humans expect it to be granted to us! And thus, it becomes the most important of all the characteristics that appear in the seeker at the fifth *Guna*.

Question
What about Buddhist? They are Shraman, and constitute its biggest branch. They are mostly non-vegetarian? Are they all flawed?

It is true that Buddhists are mostly non-vegetarian. This includes the most well-known, the most respected, the highly revered His Holiness Dalai Lama. They are Shraman, the religion that professes *Ahimsa*—the theory that advocates non-violence towards all living being. Then why are they mostly non-vegetarian?
Let's postpone this question for the moment. We will take it up again later in our discussion while contemplating on a higher *Guna's*. That time, we will be in a better situation to understand whether eating meat is in tune with the message of Buddha.

State of Shramanhood—The Boarding Pass to Godhood

6

State of Shramanhood—The Boarding Pass to Godhood

One Who Has Adopted The Great Vows (of not permitting flow of his energies in useless directions and thus) Is Equipped With All Virtuous Qualities And Good Conduct, Often Exhibits Negligence In A Manifest Or A Non-manifest Form, And Hence Whose Conduct Is A Bit Defective Is To Be Called In This (sixth) State.
—*Samansuttam Sutra*, 554

The Wise Man, Who Is Equipped With All Vows, Whose Negligence Has Disappeared Entirely, Who Remains Absorbed In Meditation, But, Who Has Started Neither Subsiding His Delusive Karmas Nor Annihilating His Delusive Karmas Is to be Called In This (seventh) State.
—Ibid., 555

FROM THIS POINT STARTS the most important phase on the path to Godhood. From here onwards, the journey enters into an overdrive mode. We discussed *Tatva*s earlier. The Figure 2.3 is a representation of a seeker who enters into this stage. Here a seeker sets aside everything that bonded him back to this *Samsara* (cycle of repeated re-births) and gets set to board the plane that would take him to Godhood.

Let's explore its various stages.

6. *Pramat Virakt* (State of Subconscious Uncontrolled)

Here, Shraman Theology further takes us into deeper layers of the human mind. On the previous ladder, *Desh Virakt*, the seeker defines boundaries of his actions, i.e. the seeker succeeds in taming his conscious mind. He does not perform any actions consciously which go against the direction he has set for himself. But the conscious mind is not the only mind that leads a person into some action or the other. The subconscious mind also controls many of our actions.

We may dictate our actions when we are awake, but we do not have any control over our self when we are asleep. Many seekers, who practice suppression of desires, actually end up dreaming all that they suppressed. The subconscious is the back door of the mind, which it uses to fulfill its desires. For example, take a person who has vowed not to get angry and suppresses his anger whenever it arises. Such a person would often press his teeth tightly in sleep or fasten his fist. He is manifesting his anger through the back door.

The *Sutra* that describes this state in *Saman Suttam* states as follows:

> *One Who Has Adopted The Great Vows, (of not permitting flow of his energies in useless directions and thus) Is Equipped With All Virtuous Qualities And Good Conduct, Often Exhibits Negligence In A Manifest Or A Non-manifest Form, And Hence Whose Conduct Is A Bit Defective Is To Be Called In This State.*
>
> Samansuttam Sutra, 554

The *Sutra* says a seeker at this stage is equipped with all virtuous qualities possible for a human, but still sometimes fails in his conduct, either visibly or invisible (i.e. in the mind or dreams).

In most cases, a seeker at this stage renounces the world and becomes a monk or a nun. But in spite of having attained monkhood, is not able to channelize his energies completely

State of Shramanhood—The Boarding Pass to Godhood 93

in the direction of Godhood and thus exhibits negligence in a manifest or a non-manifest form. Buts it's just a transitory stage. It ceases to be as the seeker evolves further and enters the seventh stage.

7. *Apramat Virakt* (State of Subconscious Controlled)

At this seventh stage, the seeker succeeds in taming his subconscious mind. Now he remains alert, when he is awake, i.e. in consciousness and also when he is asleep, i.e. in subconsciousness. This is a state of great achievement. Having tamed his subconscious, man becomes a master of his mind for the first time in the true sense of the word.

The *Sutra* that goes on describing this state is as follows:

> *The Wise Man, Who Is Equipped With All Vows, Whose Negligence Has Disappeared Entirely, Who Remains Absorbed In Meditation, But, Who Has Started Neither Subsiding His Delusive Karmas Nor Annihilating His Delusive Karmas Is to be Called In This State.*
>
> *Samansuttam Sutra*, 555

At this stage, a seeker steps into a state of raised awareness. All negligence in his day-to-day affairs disappears. His life itself becomes meditation. Now the seeker attains a state, where even basic actions of life become a meditation. Now if he walks, he walks with utmost awareness. When he talks, he talks with utmost awareness. He sits, and gets up, and even sleeps, with utmost awareness and consciousness. Or, in other words, at this stage, his subconscious mind totally ceases to exist, and he achieves cent per cent consciousness in all his actions while awake and also while asleep.

But says the *Sutra* that the seeker, at this stage, still does not start annihilating his delusive *Karmas*!

What does this *Sutra* mean by such a description? What does it actually mean by *delusive Karmas*? Has the seeker not already left all his delusive actions far behind as he entered his fifth stage of spiritual growth? Has he not already left all those *Karmas* that were wasting his energies and pulling him away from his destined Godhood? And if he has, then what is this *Sutra* now referring to as delusive *Karmas*?

To understand this delusive *Karmas* we will need to enter some of the very deep realms of Shraman Theology. As discussed earlier during the discussion of Tatva's, this school believes in the Law of *Karmas*. Law of *Karma* states action we do creates bondage for us and makes us pay back for the same. This process of bondage is referred to as *Karam-Bandh* (bondage of actions). These bondages then create for us what we call—destiny.

This is the most important precept of Shraman school. It says there is no God that creates or writes our destiny. Because if it would be so, then it really looks very mean for Him to have granted someone presidency of a country or chairmanship of a business empire and cursed someone else to be a beggar and lookout to other humans for mercy to merely survive.

This logic is one of the main reasons why the atheists have always questioned the existence of a superpower who controls the world. The Shraman school agrees to them in totality as far as the above topic of discussion is concerned. It too says that there is no God who writes our destiny. This school says—it's us. We ourselves! Based on our respective actions, creates *Karam-Bandh*.

These *Karam-Bandh* then waits for the right opportunity and right condition to come back to haunt us. And when they come, we say—it was destined.

It is this *Karam Bandh* that is referred above in the *Sutra* as Delusive *Karmas*. It's referred to as delusive because it does not appear to have been generated by us because we in our conscious mind have forgotten the actions we did in the past which are coming back.

The word used in the original Hindi text to describe delusive *Karmas* is *Mohiniya Karma*. *Mohiniya Karma* is one of the eight types of *Karam-Bandhs* that we human create for ourselves. I believe that the word *Mohiniya* is used as a symbolic of all the eight type of *Karam's* because it's the most powerful of all the eight *Karam-Bandhs* and is one of the main reasons of the falling back of a seeker from higher stages of spiritual elevation (*Gunas*) to lower rungs of its existence.

A brief discussion on these eight types of *Karam-Bandhs* and the way they hinder our onward movement will be helpful for us to understand the above *Sutra*.

The eight *Karmas* which come back, and create for us what we call our destiny are as under:

1. *Jananavaraniya Karma* (Intellect Obscuring Actions)

This *Karma-Bandh* is related to our capability to perceive and analyze. Inherently, we possess the capability to know anything and everything. This capacity of being an omniscient is one of the intrinsic properties of our soul—our real being. But this is not our state as we are today. This is because of the *Jananavarniya Karmas* that we had bound for ourselves in our past lives. It is because of bondage of this *Karma*, that our ability to know things as they are is obscured. This *Karma* decreases our intellect and ability to understand and contemplate a particular thing or object.

We bound these *Karmas* for ourselves when we were stationed at the First *Guna* of *Mithyatva* in human or lower than human forms by:

– neglecting or ridiculing learning or knowledge,
– insulting, disrespecting, harassing or hating the learned,
– remaining idle, obstructing others in their learning and by spreading incorrect information.

In the state of *Mithyatva*, when we perform such actions,

we do not realize that they will one day come back to trouble us and create obstacle for us in discovering our Godhood. But at that stage, there is no way we could have this realization either. This is precisely the reason why this stage is so much abhorred in Shraman school. The actions we commit ourselves to, at this stage makes it a filthy place to be.

If we look around ourselves, we will see a plenty of such actions happening all over. Each religion of the world, in an illusion that it's the best religion ridicules the other. Buddhists make mockery of Jains. Jews do not respect Christianity and Islam. Muslims disown all other traditions that came before Prophet Mohammad or after Him, and Hindus doubt all other traditions that arose out of India.

It's worth noting that every religion of the world helps and aims making its disciples rise above their vices and become a better human, but none of us value this endeavour. For little petty things, and in a self-gratification—ego boosting exercise, we ridicule, or insult or obstruct path of other seekers and thus end up creating for ourselves the above *Karmic* bondages.

These bondages of our past actions cloud our ability to know things as they are. After having achieved this high stage of Seventh *Guna*, these *Karmas* become an obstacle on our further elevation.

A seeker at this seventh stage when confronts these past *Karmas*, does not make any effort to annihilate them nor makes any effort to subside them and thus remains stationed at this *Guna*.

2. *Darshanavaraniya Karma* (Vision Obscuring Actions)

Like knowledge, seeing everything that exists in this world, visible, or invisible with a naked eye is also an intrinsic property of our soul. This capability of our soul remains obscured because of *Darshanavaraniya Karma* that we did while we were stationed at the First *Guna* of *Mithyatava*.

The reasons are the same as we discussed above. Actions we perform in the first *Guna* of *Mithyatva* as listed above, but which result in neglecting, ridiculing, insulting, harassing, hating or obstructing the vision of another seeker result in our creating these vision obscuring actions for us.

These bondages of our past actions cloud our ability to see things as they are. After having achieved this high stage of seventh *Guna*, these *Karmas* become an obstacle on our further elevation.

A seeker at this seventh stage when confronts these past *Karmas*, does not make any effort to annihilate these *Karmas* nor makes any effort to subside them and thus remains stationed at this *Guna*.

3. *Antaraya Karma* (Hurdle Creating Actions)

Antaraya means hurdles or obstacles. Many times we would have observed that our efforts do not result in the type of results we expected. Or otherwise we would have observed that whenever we initiate a project, we unnecessarily face unexpected difficulties. These are a result of obstacles that we bound ourselves to in our past by creating similar hurdles in the path of other persons. When these actions come back to bother us, these are referred to as *Antaraya Karma* or hurdle creating actions.

We do not need to be at the Seventh *Guna* to experience it. They come back to haunt us, as and when the time is ripe. But for a seeker at this seventh stage, since in most likelihood, he would have already moved past all material endeavours, they usually come in the form of obstacles in spiritual development. They hinder his meditation and performance of austerities and are a result of similar actions by him in the past in obstructing the path to spiritual upliftment of other seekers.

A beautiful example of what *Antaraya Karma* does is found in Buddhist annals in the story of Thera Godhika. He was a great monk and on his path to Godhood was diligently practicing Tranquility and Insight-Development, on a stone slab on the side of *Isigili Mountain* at Magadha in Bihar, India. When he had achieved one-pointedness of the mind (jhana), he became very ill; that impaired the effectiveness of his practice. In spite of his sickness, he kept on striving hard; but every time he was making some progress he was overcome by sickness. He was thus inflicted for six times. Finally, he made up his mind to overcome all obstacles and attain *Arahatship* (Godhood) even if he were to die. So, without relaxing he continued to practice diligently; in the end he decided to give up his life. At the point of death He attained *Arahatship*.[36]

This is a beautiful example of what *Antaraya Karma's* does to a seeker at this seventh stage. But a seeker who is at this stage does not make the type of efforts that *Thera Godhika* did in the above story, i.e. He does not make any effort to annihilate these *Karmas* as He did, nor makes any effort to suppress them.

4. *Mohiniya Karma* (Deluding Actions)

Mohiniya word comes from *Moh* which means attachment. *Moh* is the seed of all our vices and all our pains and sufferings. Thus this *Mohiniya Karma* is the big boss—the torchbearer among all the *Karmas* that bind our soul.

As our soul evolves in its *Atmic Cycle* from the state of one-sensed being to the state of a five-sensed being, these *Karmas* carry alongside and keep getting more and more intense with each stage of its evolution.

As we arrive in human form, we are already deeply rooted in some of these like *Veda* (desire for sex) and *Bhaya* (fear), *Shok* (sorrow) and *Krodha* (anger). And from there on, as we pass through the preliminary spiritual stages, the first stage of *Mithyatva*, the third stage of *Mishra Bhava* and the fourth stage of *Avirata Samyag Drishti*, we still keep accumulating them, though their intensity keep reducing with each rising stage. During these stages, these *Karmas* add to our *Karmic* account because of our deceitful (*Maya*), greedy (*Lobha*), proud (*Mana*), prejudiced (*Rati*), ridiculing (*Hasya*), disgustful (*Jugupsa*) and improper (*Arati*) behaviors.

Together all these actions, create for us a prison which keeps us bounded till the very last breath we take just before our enlightenment.

These collective past actions keep haunting us till we reach the tenth *Guna* (spiritual stage) leading us to perform actions which throw us back into lower realms of our spiritual existence *(Gunas)*, and manifests itself in such a horrible manner at eleventh *Guna* (spiritual stage) that they have been compared to *Satan* by various religions of the world. The *Satan* which appeared before Jesus as He approached Christhood and the *Mara* which appeared before Buddha just before His Godhood is nothing but a manifestation of these *Karmas* we sowed for ourselves in the past. We will read more of this as we discuss the eleventh *Guna* later in this discussion.

The above four *Karam-Bandh* (bondages of our past actions) initiate an action in the seeker resulting in his fall from this high point of spiritual existence and are thus further subcategorized as harming (*Ghatiya*) *Karmas*.

The balance four *Karam-Bandhs* (bondages of actions) also, following the Laws of *Karma* come back to show their effect on the seeker, but they do not initiate an action that can lead to downfall of a seeker and are thus subcategorized as Non-Harming (*Aghatiya*) *Karmas*. A brief description will help us further analyze the effect they cause on us.

5. *Ayushya Karma* (Age Deciding Actions)

Our actions that determine the age and type of life we will lead are referred to as *Ayushya* (Age Deciding) Actions. These actions determine the type of planet we will be born on, and the age we will get.

It's worth noting here that Shraman school claims that there are many more planets similar to our Earth which support human life form. Apart from these planets where humanity exists, there are several more planes of existence higher and lower than these planets where life prospers. We will discuss on all these planets and planes in following volumes of this book.

The exact planet or plane that we will be born in and the age we will have over there are decided by our *Ayushya* (age deciding) actions.

6. *Nama Karma* (Form Deciding Actions)

The actions that come back to determine the type of form we will get are refereed to as *Nama* (Form Deciding) Actions. These are the actions that determine our various physical attributes like our colour, height, physique, features and other physical attributes which make us look attractive or ugly in the eyes of our respective societies and peers.

7. *Gotra Karma* (Family Deciding Actions)

The actions which come back and decide the type of family we will be born into our refereed to as *Gotra* (Family Deciding) Actions. These *Karmas* originate on how we perceive ourselves to be in our current birth and our actions based on that perception. These are the actions that determine the race, the family, the caste and the affluence we are born into.

8. *Vedniya Karma* (Pleasure and Pain Deciding Actions)

The past actions which determine the type of pleasure and pains we will experience in our current life form are referred to as *Vedniya* (Pleasure and Pain Deciding) Actions.

When the actions we did in our past that lead to betterment of other beings come back to us, they come in the form of

Sata-Vedniya (Pleasure Giving) *Karmas* and gives us pleasures in our current life form. And when the actions we did in our past that lead to pain and anguish for other beings come back to us, they come in the form of *Asata-Vedniya* (Pain Giving) *Karmas*.

These last four *Karmas* cannot be suppressed or annihilated by the efforts of the seeker and he has no other option but to face them, till they get exhausted at his death. They do not make seeker perform an action and thus set for himself further *Karam-Bandh* (bondages of action). But the first four *Karmas* do and also set's the path of the latter four in his next life.

The path to further elevation of the soul divides into two henceforth. This difference is very subtle and needs to be fully understood as the decision we take here is going to decide whether we will reach our goal of Godhood or fall back into the lower *Gunas* we have so painstakingly moved ahead from.

In the first direction, when the *Karam-Bandhs* (bondages of our past actions) come back to bother the seeker—he, fully established in the knowledge that reacting to them will cause similar bondages in future, suppresses his desire to react. Such seeker takes the direction which is referred to as *Upsham*.

Following the second direction, when the *Karam-Bandhs* come back to bother, the seeker—he, fully understanding that it's a result of his own past actions, does not resort to any suppression, but faces it and accepts it—head-on and thus completely annihilates those past actions. Such seeker takes the direction which is referred to as *Kshapak*.

Irrespective of the direction a seeker takes, he heads on further on his spiritual elevation. But the seeker who takes the first, the *Upsham* direction is able to make it only till the eleventh *Guna* (spiritual stage) and falls back to the second

Guna from this state. All the suppressed emotions, caused because of suppressions done when the *Karam-Bandhs* came back to bother him causes this fall. We will understand why it happens as we discuss on eleventh *Guna* (spiritual stage).

The seeker who takes the second *Kshapak* direction bypasses this eleventh stage and completes his journey and attains Godhood.

A question now arises is that why does the seeker takes two such diverse paths which leads them to totally different directions? Why does a seeker who has reached a high spiritual ground as the seventh *Guna* that we are currently discussing ends up taking such varied directions.

The answer perhaps lies in the way they groomed themselves at the fourth and the fifth *Gunas* (spiritual stages). Let's spare a few moments and visit both these stages again.

At the fourth *Guna*, we discussed that the seeker at this stage has below characteristics.

> *He is Not Able to Detach Himself from Desires of Sense Organs and from Hurting of the Movable or Immovable Beings for His own Self Interests. But Still Contemplates Deeply (Shradhan) Over the Tatva's (elements) As Proclaimed by the Enlightened Masters.*

And at the fifth *Guna*, we discussed his characteristics as under:

> *One who desists from killing of mobile living beings, but not from the immobile ones like vegetation, and yet who has unwavering faith (Shradha) in the enlightened ones.*

Note the difference between the two. At the fourth *Guna*, a deep contemplation is taking place. It's a mental metamorphosis at work. The seeker is contemplating on what Jina is saying. He is logically and analytically analyzing the same. And at the fifth, this analysis ends and faith is established in what Jina has to offer.

This is very important. Faith follows reasoning. Analysis comes first, faith later. When such a chronology flows, the faith is not blind and is deeply rooted on a personal examination on what is being believed in. Now the faith does not flow out of just reverence for a person who is being believed or just out of conditioning that our society or peers have made us to believe since childhood, but is based on one's own personal rationalization and insight.

Achieving this rationalization, achieving this insight, is the most important catharsis for any soul to ensure that the faith is not just a blind belief.

A question can now be asked that if rationalization has already been done and the thing believed has already been analyzed to be true, then what is the need of faith? Faith is required for something which is too deep to be able to be proved analytically or scientifically. We do not have faith in something we have seen to be true. Because we know it's true. Say, for example, if we boil water and see it evaporating, then we know that water evaporates when boiled. We do not need to have faith that the water will evaporate when boiled.

So the question now arises is—why faith, if it needs to be preceded by reasoning?

The answer to this question lies in the topic marked to be contemplated and analyzed in the above *Sutra*—the *Tatva*. We discussed them in detail earlier.

This is the deepest knowledge. Knowledge so deep, that it's not possible for us to comprehend it completely in our current state of intellectual evolution. This is especially true for the last three *Tatvas*, viz. *Samvar, Nirjara* and *Moksha*. That is the reason faith is required. But they can be analytically analyzed. This analytical and logical evolution of the above formula (the *Tatva*) is referred to in the above *Sutra* as *Shradhan*. What follows out of this analysis is—*Shradha* or faith.

A seeker who follows this chronology, who analyzes the master formula of *Tatva* before he believe in it at the fourth *Guna*, is most likelihood to take the *Kshapak* direction as he moves ahead of the seventh *Guna*. Because after analysis of *Tatva*-knowledge, he would know why something happens, and what he needs to do, to make that not happen in future again. Thus, whenever the *Karam-Bandhs* comes back and creates a situation, where he is tempted to react, he remains centered in his self. No ripples flow in his psyche that needs to be curtailed or suppressed. This releases him from that *Karam-Bandhs*.

A seeker, who does not analytically analyze *Tatva*-knowledge at fourth *Guna* and straightaway believes in it out of his reverence to Jina or peer conditioning, is most likelihood to follow the *Upsham* direction as he moves out of seventh *Guna*. He still rises up on the ladder to Godhood as he is following the right path of spiritual elevation. But now, since he has not analyzed the *Tatva* and blindly believed in the same, when the *Karam-Bandhs* creates situations, where he is tempted to react, ripples of emotions rise in his psyche. Because of lack of understanding of *Tatva*-knowledge, instead of facing that situation and annihilating that past misdeed, he resorts to suppression of those mental ripples to escape out of it and thus treads the *Upsham* direction.

Before we proceed, another very important thing that needs to be noted is that the path onwards from this point, irrespective of the direction (*Upsham* or *Kshapak*) taken by the seeker is not like a ladder like the *Guna's* we have discussed till now. It's rather like a pole where a seeker cannot rest.

This needs to be understood. All the *Gunas* we discussed earlier are places where a seeker can rest and remain stationed for long periods of his *Atmic Cycle* (except for the second and third). But henceforth, it's not the case unless the seeker has achieved his Godhood. As the seeker moves ahead from seventh stage, he would either need to surpass all the balance Guna's and attain Godhood, or will need to come back and rest again at the seventh or a lower stage. In this process of rising up to higher *Gunas* and coming back, the seeker will pass and experience the characteristics and fragrances of each higher state, but cannot station himself at that state permanently and will either need to complete his journey or comeback to this seventh state, or fall further down into lower states of spiritual elevation.

Let's keep this in mind as we proceed further on understand the balance higher states of a being.

Discussion

- We discussed earlier that Shraman Theology puts a great importance on intellect. It was referred to as *Pragya*—a state of mind where having understood that something is unworthy gets denounced automatically and the action is not undertaken. Then why is it that vows are required to be taken at this stage and such a great importance is given to them that *Guna* depends on whether they are being followed completely or not?
- Can a seeker rise to these stages of sixth and seventh *Gunas* without becoming a monk?

Question

We discussed earlier that Shraman Theology puts a great importance on intellect. It was referred to as Pragya—a state of mind where having understood that something is unworthy gets denounced automatically and the action is not undertaken. Then why is it that vows are required to be taken at this stage and such a great importance is given to them that Guna depends on weather they are being followed completely or not?

Pragya (intellect) indeed is central to Shraman Theology, as no advancement in spiritual life is possible without it. It is in and around *Pragya*, that the ladder to Godhood gets erected. The question is—then why should one take vows? A vow is a promise, a self-disciplinary mechanism of doing something and not doing something. The question is if intellect itself is firm, if a seeker is fully established in his *Pragya*, then by itself he will do only the worthwhile actions and fordo the unworthy. What's the need to take vows?

The answer to this question perhaps lies in human psychology. We humans are such that our mind wavers. It oscillates like a pendulum. From one extreme to another! And this oscillation is such that more extreme it hits in one direction, greater is the force it acquires to do the opposite. As the seeker rises higher on the spiritual elevation, greater is the possibilities of his encountering spiritual highs. We will discuss these spiritual highs in the next chapter. And with each spiritual high, the possibility of mind doing a somersault increases accordingly.

And this perhaps is the reason that vows are required. To ensure that we do not fall back into the old habits which we, through our *Pragya* has already known as unworthy.

Taking vows helps us ensure that. It adds more strength to the *Pragya*. Just as we add cement around the columns of steel to ensure that the building we construct is strong, the same way vows are taken to further strengthen the *Pragya* and ensure a strong foundation on which the castle of a spiritual high could be built. Just as a building cannot be build just on steel columns, or just on cement, similarly, the elevation to Godhood cannot take place just based on *Pragya* or just based on vows. A combination of both is essential to ensure this flowering.

Question

Can a seeker rise to these stages of sixth and seventh Gunas without becoming a monk?

Sixth and the seventh stages are supposed to be the stages of a monk or a nun. Someone who has renounced the material world completely! Thus, as per this analysis, one can reach these high stages only after renouncing the world. However, this is not a thumb rule.

The following *Sutra* of Jina confirms the same. The *Sutra* says:-

Though In General, Monks (and nuns) Well Established In Right Character Are Better In Sanyam (self restrain) Than Householders, But There are Few Monks (and nuns) From Whom Householders Are better In Sanyam (self restrain).
—Samansutam Sutra, 298

Thus, as per this *Sutra,* it can well be established that a householder, who has fully understood the knowledge of *Tatvas* and has started using this master formula for his betterment can also raise himself to these high points through self-restraining his actions and channelizing them in right direction. A direction where he ends up plugging the arrival of new *Karmas* and annihilation of the old!

Experiences of Apurvakarana—Arrival of ESPs

7

Experiences of Apurvakarana— Arrival of ESPs

In This Stage of Spiritual Development the Soul Experiences Unique but Frequently Changing Mental States of Bliss Which Have Not Been Experienced Ever Before: Hence the Stage is Called Apurvakarana.
—*Samansuttam Sutra*, 556

8. *Apurvakarana* (State of Bliss)

THIS IS A STAGE WHERE the seeker and his life transform forever. The seeker ceases to be a person of this world. He becomes a messenger from beyond. He gets connected to some other world. He attains a state of never before experienced pleasure and ecstasy. He attains a state of Bliss.

This is perhaps the stage where one experiences *Samadhi*—a transcendental state of mind that occurs only when a seeker attains a state of no-mind. Patanjali has called it *Rising of Kundalini*—awakening of ones cosmic powers. Dadu says it's like experiencing thousands of suns together. Sufis have said that it's a state where one experiences *Anhad Naad*—the music of the Divine.[1]

Something new starts happening. Something which the person has never experienced in his life or it's better to say in all the lives he had lived so far in his *Atmic Cycle*. The *Sutra* that describes this state is as follows:

In This Stage of Spiritual Development the Soul Experiences Unique but Frequently Changing Mental States of Bliss Which Have Not Been Experienced Ever Before: Hence the Stage is Called Apurvakarana.

—*Samansuttam Sutra*, 556

Apurvakarana literally means happening of something that has never happened before. Is this the state where the seeker attains psychic powers? Perhaps yes. *Patanjali* has referred to a long list of psychic experiences which the seeker may experience. It includes experiences like rising above ground during meditation, to turning of one's blood from red to white. Chinese Tao also describes such experiences in different *Sutras*. It calls these experiences as "treasures of the inner world" and claims that just like the treasures of the outer world, it is something that needs to be renounced by the seeker of liberation.[9] Patanjali agrees, and says that an expression of such powers is dangerous, and could become a hindrance in further progression of a Soul on spiritual ladder.[1]

But does anything like the above actually happen? Are there really any psychic powers? Buddha and Christ were supposed to have these. They could heal any person of any disease just by their touch! The Jina also often referred to a state of "*Jati-Samran-Gyan*"—acquiring knowledge of many of one's past lives, i.e. a state of mind where a seeker recollects all that he has been in all his previous lives.

Buddha also referred to a similar state while answering to a question of Ajatasattu, emperor of Magdha—the most prosperous state of the golden days of Indian history. Ajatasattu was a very materialist man and believed little in the gospel of *Moksha* or *Nirvana* as professed by Buddha and His contemporaries. So he asked Buddha of the benefits of accepting monkhood—here and now, that can be seen and experienced. He was not interested in the benefits one get beyond—after death. For him the benefits one get "here and now", in this world were all that matters. In answer Buddha referred to a state of *Jati-Samran-Gyan*. The answer is registered in *Samaññaphala Sutta* and states as under:

> *With his mind thus concentrated, purified, and bright, unblemished, free from defects, pliant, malleable, steady, and attained to imperturbability, he directs and inclines it to knowledge of the recollection of past lives (lit: previous homes). He recollects his manifold past lives, i.e., one birth, two births, three births, four, five, ten, twenty, thirty, forty, fifty, one hundred, one thousand, one hundred thousand, many aeons of cosmic contraction, many aeons of cosmic expansion, many aeons of cosmic contraction and expansion, [recollecting], 'There I had such a name, belonged to such a clan, had such an appearance. Such was my food, such my experience of pleasure and pain, such the end of my life. Passing away from that state, I re-arose there. There too I had such a name, belonged to such a clan, had such an appearance. Such was my food, such my experience of pleasure and pain, such the end of my life. Passing away from that state, I re-arose here.' Thus he recollects his manifold past lives in their modes and details.*

Such a state of remembrance of past lives can occur at any *Gunas*, but there is a very great possibility of this happening at this eighth stage.

This is so because all that we tend to forget consciously actually gets buried in our subconscious mind. And if the theory of reincarnation of soul or subtle mind is true, then all that we have forgotten about our past lives would be laying buried in our subconscious. And if at the seventh stage of Subconscious Controlled (*Apramat Virakt*), the seeker has become aware of his subconscious mind, then he ought to also become aware of all of his forgotten experiences of the past. Of this life and the other lives he has lived so far. All twenty-four Shraman Great Masters were supposed to have this knowledge. So did Buddha. So did many more saints of this world.

The question now arises that if there are any such powers, then why has it been advised to the seeker not to use it? Why Buddha and Patanjali and Lao-Tzu have all warned their disciples against using it? After all if they exist, they could be used for the betterment of this world!

Probably, the reason of it is that it is not the betterment of world that is important for a seeker. Rather, it is betterment of self, or betterment of one's own soul.

The inherent risk in using these powers is that they could become binding. More binding than the treasures of the outer world! The reason is that the seeker would then be tempted to use it for the sake of the others and thus might feel that he is doing something good. But, in reality, he would be doing all this for the gratification of his own self and for telling the world about his great height and achievements in the spiritual world.

This would create a very dangerous subtle ego, which would become very difficult to renounce for the rest of his life. And if such a seeker dies after having attained this stage, *Patanjali* says that he will be born back with psychic powers inherent in him and without any knowledge of where it came from and what he is supposed to do with them.[2]

There are many people who have been identified by the Western nations who have such powers but without any knowledge of where it came from. One of the most famous persons with such inborn powers was Nostradamus—the man who saw the future and wrote a lot of prophecies, many of which have been found to be true. Modern science calls such powers as ESPs—Extra Sensory Perceptions and considers it a natural gift.

During the Cold War, there was a separate department of

USA's secret service—CIA, who used the help of such people to know what was happening behind the iron curtain of the Soviet Union. Many things that were told by these people were found true after the end of Cold War.[11] Soviet Union had its own stories about such people. There was extensive research carried out on them by the communists. In fact, they described it as the "Ultimate Weapon" against their enemy.[12] They were very scientific in their attitude and unlike other Western nations did not believe that they were God-gifted. They believed neither in God nor in any God-gifts. Their attitude towards such powers was simple—if it's possible for one human, it is possible for all.

As per Shraman Theology, they were correct. It's possible for all humans. But as Lao-Tzu pointed out, it's just a stage that one achieves during his spiritual elevation, and must be passed on and moved over from.

Discussion

- The above state looks more like a fairy tale. How do we believe in it?
- The remembrance of past lives as consciousness breaks into the subconscious looks logical. But what about other ESPs like seeing what's happening thousands of miles away or foreseeing the future or reading other's mind! What's the logic behind acquiring such powers?

Question
The above state looks more like a fairy tale. How do we believe in it?

From here onwards, the higher we raise on the *Gunas*; we will experience many more similar fairytale-like things. But it's not our mistake. It's a result of our limited vision. At the point we are, we have our own limitations of sight. But the higher we keep getting on the *Gunas*, this limitation keeps eroding and our vision keeps increasing.

It's similar to our capability to visualize things as we start ascending a mountain. As we keep getting higher, our capability to visualize the objects not visual from lower planes keeps rising. Similarly, when we reach higher *Gunas*, our ability to visualize these higher stages increases.

But this does not mean that we should accept them blindly. An analytical and logical analysis of the same is must. That's what we intended to do in our past discussion and will continue to do so as we enter the even more mystical higher stages we will discuss ahead.

Question

The remembrance of past lives as consciousness breaks into the subconscious looks logical. But what about other ESPs like seeing what's happening thousands of miles away or foreseeing the future or reading other's mind! What's the logic behind acquiring such powers?

It's very difficult to answer this question, because it's a topic beyond metal contemplation. That's why most of us tend to mark these powers as "God-gift". But we now know that, it's not God-gift, and that they are just an after-effect of a stage, which a seeker passes through during his evolution to Godhood.

If we try to find a logical reasoning to it, then perhaps it lies in the way our vital energies behave at this high point of our spiritual upliftment.

At the lower *Gunas* these energies keep flowing outwards into the outer world because of our vices like anger, greed, sensual desires and other animalistic passions. But as the seeker rises higher, he slowly and gradually starts cutting down the outward flow of these energies. By the time he reaches the seventh *Guna*, the level of his awareness raises so high, that almost every non-required action, both physically and mentally ceases to be.

Perhaps it's these unutilized energies that gets transformed into raising the capability of our sense organs to high points that we refer today as ESPs—The Extra Sensory Perceptions. But it's just contemplation. To the best of my knowledge, there is no such analysis or reasons given in *Jain Agams* (sacred texts).

But we do find a reference to these in *Yogic* and *Tantric* texts. They refer to existence of seven *chakras* in our body.[2] The position of these *chakras* is perfectly in tune with the existence of our vital glands as described by modern science.

As per these *Yogic* and *Tantric* texts, when the human lives at lower levels of consciousness, his energies reside at the lower most *chakra*—the root *chakra* and flows out in the form of various animalistic vices we discussed above. But as the seeker move upwards to higher consciousness, the energies also rise above to higher *chakras* resulting in these ESPs.

Perhaps we can get a clue from these explanations as to why ESPs occur at this eighth stage of spiritual elevation.

Anter-mhurhat—Last Forty-eight Minutes to Godhood

8

Anter-mhurhat—Last Forty-eight Minutes to Godhood

The Souls Occupying The Ninth Stage Of Spiritual Development Enjoy The Constant Mental State Each Moment And Burns Down The Forest Of Karmas Through The Flames Of The Fire Of A Very Pure Meditation Are Called Anivrttikarna.
—Samansuttam Sutra, 558

Just As A Kusumbha Flower Has A Slight Tinge Of Reddish Color, Similarly A Monk Who Has Reached This Tenth Stage Of Spiritual Development Retains A Slight Tinge Of Attachment Internally. Hence This Stage Is Called Suksham Kasaya or Suksham Sampray, i.e. The Stage of Slight Attachment.
—Samansuttam Sutra, 559

Just As Water Mixed With Kataka-Fruit, Or Water of a Lake in Winter Season Appears Clean & Fresh, Similarly is a State of A Seeker at This Stage of Upshant Moh Who has Subdued All His Delusive Karmas (actions).
—Samansuttam Sutra, 560

HERE WE REACH THE culmination, the climax of the entire spiritual upliftment we have been discussing till now. The Godhood is now just Forty-eight minutes away, a time span named as *Anter-mhurhat* in Jain Theology. And this is also the most difficult part of the journey or perhaps the easiest one too. It depends on seeker to seeker, and the way he molded himself in the preliminary stages of spiritual evolution (the lower *Gunas* we discussed earlier).

(9) *Anivrttikarna* (State of Transcendence)
What happens hense? Transcendence! A seeker moves above society and religion. Till now, in all likelihood, a seeker must have been following one path or the other of spirituality, shown by one or the other Great Master. He may be following Patanjali's *Yoga Sutras*, or may be following instructions of Buddha, or Jesus, or any other Great Master. He might have been either a Hindu, or a Muslim, or a Christian, or might have been following any other sect. But at this point of transcendence, he ceases to be any of the above and moves beyond. He rises above religion and attains true Humanity. This is the point where Buddha, in spite of having born into a Hindu family, ceased to be a Hindu. This is the point, where Jesus in spite of having born into a Jew family, ceased to be a Jew.[1]

This is the point, when a seeker transcends his religion. But why does it happen? Why does the path, that the seeker has been following, and that has led him so far in his spiritual quest, suddenly becomes less important and the seeker is forced to move beyond?

The reason perhaps is that since childhood, a society starts conditioning a person. Society deliberately or not, starts inculcating in a child its own values and beliefs. If it believes in God, it starts teaching the same to the child. And, if it believes in No-God, then it starts teaching the same. But all these beliefs are only myopic views, a much smaller part of a great reality!

This can be better understood by taking an example of the visibility of a person standing on the ground and comparing it to the visibility of the person who has climbed a tree top. Just like, by climbing a higher platform, a person start getting a better view of reality, similar is the state of a person who is elevated to a higher level of spiritual development. Now the seeker comes to a point where he realizes that the truth is much deeper than what he originally thought and tries to add on or refine the old beliefs. But, in doing that, he seems to stand against what the society originally believes in and thus appear to be spreading a new message.

This is the reason that such seekers are either killed by society or a new religion comes forth. But, in reality, there is nothing new. It's the same old message—just coming in through a new source. From someone who is close to reaching the beyond or has already realized the beyond.

And since such a person is born in an age that is different from his predecessor, his techniques and teachings also appear to be different. This is the reason that a new religion stands behind him. But people, who have vision, realize that there is nothing new. It's just the same old wine in a new bottle. Early Christians must have been such visionaries. Probably, that is the reason behind calling the compilation of Jesus' teachings—New Testament—an extension of the Old Testament!

The seeker, at this stage attains the same state of mind as that of a person, when he is born. Free from all conditionings of the society. This is probably why Jesus said that only those people would be permitted in the Kingdom of His Father, who would be just like a child. Jesus probably was referring to this ninth stage of spiritual growth because attaining a state like that of child is not possible, until a seeker is de-conditioned of all the partial truths that he has been fed since his childhood.

The *Sutra* that describes the seeker at this stage is as follows:

The Souls Occupying The Ninth Stage Of Spiritual Development Enjoy The Constant Mental State Each Moment And

Burns Down The Forest Of Karmas Through The Flames Of The Fire Of A Very Pure Meditation Are Called Anivrttikarna.
—*Samansuttam Sutra,* 558

Such beings, says the *Sutra,* attain a constant mental state. Unlike the seeker at the eighth state, who experiences frequently changing mental states, a seeker at this state matures and attains a constant state of Bliss. Probably, it's just like the experiences attained while climbing a mountain or going to a hill station. As the person starts climbing higher, and starts moving away from the heat of the plains, he starts feeling the coolness of the mountains. This coolness and the refreshing experience start getting more and more profound as he keeps getting close to his destination. However, when he reaches the destination, his experiences become constant.

Similarly, a seeker till attaining this ninth state keeps getting newer and more profound experiences of his inner self, but after having achieved it, his experience gets constant, or he settles in himself completely. A ripple that started in his psyche as he stepped out of the first state of *Mithyatva*—which grew into a great tsunami of constantly changing mental states at the eighth state of *Apurvakarana*; now, comes to a rest and a seeker attains a state of meditation of a very pure nature. This state of mind engrossed in deep one-pointed meditation, burns down the forest of his past *Karmas* (actions).

(10) *Suksham Sampray* (Reflexes Uncontrolled)

The tenth stage of spiritual development is *Suksham Sampray*. The *Sutra* that describes the seeker at this stage is as follows:

Just As A Kusumbha Flower Has A Slight Tinge Of Reddish Color, Similarly A Monk Who Has Reached This Tenth Stage Of

Spiritual Development Retains A Slight Tinge Of Attachment Internally. Hence This Stage Is Called Suksham Kasaya or Suksham Sampray, i.e. The Stage of Slight Attachment.
—*Samansuttam Sutra,* 559

The *Sutra* says that at this stage, the seeker has moved beyond all his active desires, but still in his passive mind there does exist, a slight tinge of desires.

Now this is something to be understood and scientifically analyzed. A seeker has reached his tenth stage of spiritual development. Of the fourteen, only four more are left to attain, and still Shraman Theology says that there does exist, a slight tinge of attachment.

Moreover, attachments and desires and love and hate are all the byproducts of the mind! It is mind that loves or feels love, it is mind that hates and it is mind that desires. As per Shraman Theology, the minds—both conscious and subconscious- have been left far behind! As per the fourteen spiritual stages, a seeker enters his sixth stage of *Pramat Virakt* only after he has controlled his conscious mind and the seeker enters the seventh stage of *Apramat Virakt* only after he has transcended his subconscious mind.

Now, when both conscious and sub-conscious minds have already been overpowered, then how is it possible that there are other leftovers or byproducts of the mind? This could be because of two reasons. First reason is that in spite of having moved beyond his conscious and subconscious minds, there is still the possibility that a seeker may fall back to the desires of mind. The second reason is that apart from the conscious and subconscious minds, there is another layer of mind far deeper than the earlier two. Psychologists call this third layer as reflexes.

The first reason can be understood by the following example.[1] Consider a floor where water has been flowing for some time. Now if the sources of water are stopped, the floor will eventually dry up. Water will cease to exist from the floor but still dry traces of water will be present. There is every possibility that if the source of water is again opened, then the water will start flowing again on the same old dried up traces. Similarly, it is possible that a seeker, specially the one who has taken the *Upsham* direction and renounced the worldly pleasures, may have attained all the spiritual heights just by plugging all the sources of desires but still there may be some dry traces of desire left over in his mind. Now, there is every possibility that if the sources of desire get unplugged somehow, then he may again slip into the same old habits.

A story in Buddhist Annals about a nun called Saccatapavi further highlights such a state. The story is as under:

A white robed nun who lived in a hut in a cemetery near Benares (Banaras) and abstained from four out of every five meals she was held in high esteem.

On a certain festival day, some goldsmiths were seated in a tent making merry. One of them, becoming sick through drink, vomited, saying: "Praise be to Saccatapāvī."

One of the others called him a fool, saying that all women were alike, and accepted a wager of one thousand that he would seduce Saccatapāvī.

The next day he disguised himself as an ascetic and stood near her hut, worshipping the sun. Saccatapāvī saw him and worshipped him, but he neither looked at her nor spoke. On the fourth day, he greeted her, and on the sixth day, as she stood near him, they talked of the penances they practiced, and the ascetic professed that his were far more severe than hers. But he confessed that he had found no spiritual calm; neither had she and they agreed that it would be better to return to and enjoy the lay life.

He brought her to the city and having lain with her and made her drunk, he handed her over to his friends.

—*The Jataka*

What happened? A nun who was practising a very virtuous life, slipped when she was offered what she had abstained. As soon as the opportunity to fulfill the plugged in desires arrived, she slithered. The above story explains the first reason.

Second reason could be that of reflexes. A seeker may initiate into an action that is caused by reflexes. Modern science would perhaps totally agree to it.

Today, scientists say that a reflex action is not initiated by the mind. In fact, the mind gets to know about the action after it has happened, even though the action is already initiated.

What is it that causes these reflex actions? It is caused by the most subtle and basic desires. At the root, one such desire is the desire to live. And it is for this reason that the reflexes act the most. This desire catches our mind the earliest on its progression from a state of a being with just one sense organ like amoeba to what we are today. What Darwin called the theory of evolution; the Indian spiritual mystics have called the evolution of soul or evolution of mind. As the soul progresses, from basic forms of life to higher, so does its mind. Or, in other words, the progression of the soul is actually the progression of the mind. From beings with no mind, the soul develops into beings with reflexes, to beings with conscious and subconscious minds.

Today, modern science divides living forms into two—intelligent living forms and unintelligent living forms. Today, when scientists ponder over the question of possibility of life on other planets, the next question that strikes them is the possibility of an intelligent life on other planets. And I think that the only difference between the intelligent and unintelligent life forms is that the unintelligent life forms are the beings in which the mind has still not evolved above the state of reflexes.

Since in the evolution of life, this state comes much earlier than the state of intelligent life form, therefore, reflexes can be called a much older layer than the conscious and subconscious layers of mind. And since this layer is much older and much deeper, it is also more mundane than the upper two. This explains the reason why reactions caused because of it in the body are caused by far more basic desires like the desire to live.

There is an interesting story from the life of Buddha that highlights how much reflexes control us. Once a big stone came rolling down from the hill, right towards the Buddha and his disciples. It had been thrown down by his cousin who was very jealous of Him and wanted to kill Him. Seeing the stone coming, all the disciples of Buddha ran for their life, but Buddha did not move. Luckily, the stone passed off just by His side, only hurting his toe.

What happened in this incident? All the disciples of Buddha ran away. They forgot Buddha. They must have come to Buddha because of the desire for spiritual growth, but this desire for spiritual growth is also the desire of the conscious and subconscious minds. However, the reflexes proved much more powerful than those desires and made them run away. All the disciples who ran away must have been either on or below this tenth stage of spiritual development as they still reacted to the desires of reflexes. But why was there no reaction in Buddha? Because He is a Buddha! Someone who has moved beyond reflexes! Some one who has conquered reflexes too! He had moved beyond this tenth stage of *Suksham Sampray*.

(11) *Upshant Moh* (The Last Battle)

The last battle! Over what? Against what? For what? Answers are—Over Oneself, Against Oneself and For Oneself. Over one's own mind that desires! Against one's own mind that is filled with passions and hate and greed and lust! And for one's own soul, to realize one's own self, to attain one's own freedom from the cycle of birth and death, for attaining one's own Godhood. This is the last step. The last frontier between manhood and Godhood!

But what exactly happens at this stage? A seeker at this stage, by burning all his desires (of conscious, subconscious and reflexes), attains a state like an enlightened master, but for only some time. The *Sutra* that describes this state says as under:

> *Just As Water Mixed With Kataka-Fruit, Or Water of a Lake in Winter Season Appears Clean & Fresh, Similarly is a State of A Seeker at This Stage of Upshant Moh Who has Subdued All His Delusive Karmas (actions).*
> —Samansuttam Sutra, 560

The *Sutra* says that a seeker at this stage can be compared to water mixed with *Kataka-fruit* or the water of a lake in the winter season. This comparison needs to be understood.

Mixing Kataka-seeds to water is the traditional Indian technique of purifying water when all the modern amenities of distilling water were not available. The World Health Organization mentions the existence of this technique in India and also recommends it to countries where modern systems of purifying water are non-existent. Jina compares a seeker at this stage to water mixed with Kataka-fruit seeds to achieve purity.

In the second simile, He compares it to the water of a lake in winter season. Since in winter the water of a lake is very cold; so no one goes near the lake. As a result of no-moment in the lake, the dirt in it subsides and the water appears clean and fresh.

It's worth noting that in both similes, the comparison of a seeker has been made to something that appears very pure, but actually still has dirt or impurities in it. In the first case, the impurities exist in the form of the Kataka-seeds and in the second, it still lies buried in the bed of the lake.

Similar says Jina, is the state of a seeker at this stage. He appears pure and clean, just like an enlightened master, but actually deep inside, he still has certain desires leftover. Just as until Kataka-seeds are removed the water cannot be called pure and just as by any moment in the lake the dirt accumulated at its bed is bound to come up, similarly a seeker at this stage still runs the risk of falling back into the trap of his desires and passions.

Now how is this possible? A seeker has already overpowered all the known layers of mind. He has already mastered the art of controlling his conscious, subconscious and reflexes. Now how is it possible that his desires could still reign supreme and initiate him into the trap of actions for gratification of his desires? This *Sutra* requires more intellection.

This happens because there is another level of mind. Even beyond reflexes which may cause a reaction in us. Modern science is yet to discover it. But Shraman Theology gives a hint of its existence at this eleventh stage of spiritual elevation. I would want to name that last level as "The Last Mind". Last because there is no mind left beyond it! This is the last level! The mind is conquered after this level, in totality. With all its passions and desires, completely! But before that, it will try to come back to power with one last battle. It knows that the three frontiers—the conscious, the subconscious, and the reflexes have already been conquered, and that if it loses this last frontier, it will die. So, it will again try and initiate the seeker, back into the actions, and for that, it will throw open the doors of all those possibilities, that the seeker may have desired in his entire *Atmic Cycle*.

There is a story in Hindu scriptures, of sage Vishwamitra. He was about to achieve enlightenment. This became a threat for the King of Heaven—the Indra and he decided to send in one of his nymphs—Meneka, to seduce the sage. Meneka succeeded, and brought the sage down from his Spiritual Heights. This probably, is a story of a seeker, on the eleventh stage of spiritual development.

Scientifically, this story can be analyzed as under.[1] *Indra* means the master of *Indris* (Sanskrit word meaning senses), i.e. master of senses—the Mind! And, whenever, a seeker is about to attain enlightenment, the dominance of mind over the seeker gets endangered. Normally, the seeker, for ages had lived as a slave of his own mind. Since the time, the seeker started on his journey of spiritual upliftment, he had been challenging the dominance of his mind. Slowly and gradually, the seeker has conquered his conscious, subconscious, and reflexive mind. Now, the mind is in danger. Now the dominance of the master of senses, the mind—the *Indra* is in danger. Its dominance over the seeker is about to end forever. So the mind sends in objects of the seeker's most subtle desires. This desire, in this case, must have been a woman—prettiest in the world, in fact of beyond—of heavens, a nymph. And the last mind, in its last battle, threw open the possibility of realizing that dream and initiated the seeker, back into the actions of this world.

Is this story true? Did any such thing really happen? Or did it take place just in a dream? Perhaps for a seeker at this stage, it really does not make any difference. People who know, say this world is a *Mithya*—a dream. And if this world, which is so real, can be a dream, then certainly a dream can also be as real as this world? But even if this story is false, it does send out a very subtle message, a message of the last battle. The war at the last frontier! And this story of Vishwamitra is not the only one that touches upon this last battle. In fact, there are similar stories across almost all the religions of the world.

When Gautama, the Buddha was about to attain enlightenment, then Mara—the *Satan* appeared and tried to tempt Him. But Gautama moved beyond to attain Buddhahood. There is a similar story about Jesus as well. *Satan* is also supposed to have appeared and offered him the empire of this entire world and all its wealth and the most beautiful women. But Jesus also moved on to become Christ.[1]

There has to be some truth in all these stories. And perhaps that truth is "The Last Mind". It's called the King of Heavens, the master of senses in the first and *Mara* or *Satan*—the Bad Mind in the other two. But it's the same "last mind". The Buddha's interaction with this last mind called Mara in Buddhist annals is worth taking a note. The story is as under:

> *Mara manifested himself in the guise of a ploughman, carrying a large plough on his shoulder, holding a long goad stick, his hair disheveled, wearing hempen garments, his feet smeared with mud. He approached The Buddha and said to Him: "May be you've seen my oxen, ascetic?"*

The word oxen here are meant to symbolize the sense organs and sensual objects.

> *Buddha having realized this meaning said "What are oxen to you, evil one?" On hearing this counter question Mara rebuked Buddha saying "The eye is mine, ascetic, forms are mine, eye-contact and its base of consciousness are mine. Where can you go, ascetic to escape from me?"*

The above words of Mara are worth noting. He says eyes are mine, i.e. he owns them. Then Mara says forms are mine, i.e. he owns the sensual objects too. Furthermore Mara says eye-contact is mine, i.e. it's in his power to decide what all forms or object of senses the eyes will see. And thereafter Mara says the base of consciousness where the eye-contact touches the body is mine too, i.e. the power to decide how to perceive what is being looked at is also mine. Or, in other words Mara claims control over all senses, sense objects and the sensual desires and ridicules Buddha and says "where can you go ascetic, to escape from me?"

The Mara in the above Buddhist annals is similar to Indra in the Hindu annals—the master of senses—The mind.

The answer of Buddha to Mara above is also worth writing in gold. Buddha says:

"The eye is yours, evil one, forms are yours, eye-contact and its base of consciousness are yours, but evil one, where there is no eye, no form, no eye-contact and its base of consciousness—there is no place for you there, evil one!"

Buddha has settled Himself at a place which was deeper than the mind. Or, in other words, he has transcended mind and thus gained control over it. He has settled Himself at a place where mind ceased all its powers over Him and could no longer tempt him to follow its dictates.

It is this last layer of mind that Jina is referring to in the above *Sutra* as the eleventh stage of spiritual development—*Upshant Moh*. *Upshant* means "The most subtle", and *Moh* means attachment or desire, i.e. the most subtle of attachments or desires of mind, in its entire *Atmic Cycle*. And, until the seeker moves beyond it, he is still away from Godhood; still a part of this world, still caught in the cycle of birth and death and may fall back, into the most mundane rung of the fourteen stages of progression of his Soul.

This is why, the Shraman Theology has recommended that once a seeker achieves the seventh stage of Subconscious Controlled (*Apramat Virakt*), he should take the *Kshapak* direction, so that the possibility of losing this battle is reduced.

Before we proceed further, there is another dimension that needs to be discussed of this eleventh stage. As per Jain Theology, this state is a dead-end in further development of a soul.

Now, what does that mean?

As per Jain Theology, for a seeker who trains his mind well, this state never arrives on his elevation to Godhood and after tenth stage, he jumps over it straight onto the next twelfth stage of *Kshin Moh*. And if this does not happen, and Mara appears, then there is no escape from it. It's all too powerful, and similar to Sage Vishwamitra, the seeker has no other option, but to fall back, into the most mundane of *Gunas* (spiritual stages).

But how does this statement explain the case of Buddha and Jesus? How do we explain their escape from the clutches of the Last Mind? Out of my reverence for them, I would like to call it an exception. Exceptions do occur and there are such instances in Jain Theology where things happened that as per normal Shraman Theology do not occur. So unlike most of my brothers in faith, I would like to believe that both Buddha and Jesus did transcend this stage and moved on to the twelfth stage of *Kshin Moh* to discover their Godhood.

Normally, Jains find it difficult to equate Buddha to Jina. Equating Jesus to Him will be all the more difficult especially because He ate meat. As per the above chronology of *Gunas* (spiritual elevation), turning vegetarian is an essential to achieve the fifth *Guna* of *Desh Virakt*.

Let's recall the *Sutra* that defined a seeker at fifth stage. It said:

> "One who desists from killing of mobile living beings, but not from the immobile ones like vegetation, and yet who has unwavering faith (Shradha) in the enlightened ones."

Jesus certainly did not mind eating the killed mobile living beings. On the contrary, He promoted non-vegetarian food. I would like to quote certain verses from Bible as under:

> "What goes into a man's mouth does not make him 'unclean,' but what comes out of his mouth, that is what makes him 'unclean.'"
>
> Matthew 15:11

> "Are you so dull?" he asked. "Don't you see that nothing that enters a man from the outside can make him 'unclean'?
>
> Mark 7:18

> For it doesn't go into his heart but into his stomach, and then out of his body."
>
> Mark 7:19

The difference between the above *Sutra* of Jina on non killing and the above verses from Bible needs to be understood. Jina says a seeker on achieving the fifth Guna restrains himself from killing mobile living beings. This comes out of a heart which is filled with compassion for all living forms of life. Turning vegetarian is just a reflection of it which follows by itself after a seeker becomes more sensitive of his actions and it's after-effects on other sentient beings.

Jesus too places more importance on keeping a pure heart in the above verses. Once the heart is clean, it too would lead to the concept of *Ahimsa* (theory of live and let live) by default.

But why did it not happen with Jesus? Why did He keep feeding Himself to meat till the last supper He had with His disciples.

Perhaps the reason is that Jesus was connected to the Tibetan Buddhist School where eating meat is allowed. This is as per a theory that Jesus had spent missing years of his youth (aged twelve to thirty of which Church has no account) in India in the company of Tibetan lamas. This theory is based on writings of Notovitch, a European traveller who was supposed to have seen some annals at the monastery of Hemis near Leh. He declared that he has seen old Buddhist Annals that had reference of Christ having lived and studied with them before he left back for Jerusalem. As per this theory, Christianity becomes an extension of Tibetan Buddhism.

Christian Church dismissed Notovitch claims immediately calling it his own invention to gain publicity.

This debate can carry on later, but another question that arises here is what about the non-vegetarian tradition in Buddhism. Whether Christ picked up this tradition from Tibetan Buddhist or not, but Tibetan Buddhists are a part of Shraman tradition without doubt. And if vegetarianism is the central most philosophy of Shraman School, then how do we explain the widespread non-vegetarianism in Buddhism which in turn is the largest branch of Shraman school of thought? We pondered over this question earlier too. Now let's try and get an answer to it.

This resulted out of an incident. Once a Buddhist monk was begging alms and an eagle dropped a loaf of meat into his begging bowl. Buddha had set a rule that monks should not eat meat and another rule that one should accept whatever was offered to him. This created confusion and the monk came to Buddha on what should he do. Buddha went into a deep contemplation and then permitted monk to eat whatever has been offered in his bowl.

A great catastrophe befell the Shraman School that day. The above incident was taken as permission from Buddha to eat meat if it was offered to them as long as they do not indulge in killing themselves. Buddha probably felt that dropping of meat in the monk's bowl by an eagle is a one off incident and will never occur again. But now it happens daily. The only difference is that now it's dropped by lay followers in the begging bowls and monks keep eating the same.

Buddha probably realized His mistake later. On the very eve of His death, in the *Mahaparinirvana Sutra*, which are regarded as the final elucidatory and definitive Mahayana teachings of the Buddha, He states that "the eating of meat extinguishes the seed of Great Kindness", adding that all and every kind of meat and fish consumption (even of animals found already dead) is prohibited by Him.

He specifically rejects the idea that monks who go out begging and receive meat from a donor should eat it. He says:

". . . it should be rejected . . . I say that even meat, fish, game, dried hooves and scraps of meat left over by others constitutes an infraction . . . I teach the harm arising from meat-eating."

The Buddha also predicts in this *Sutra* that later monks will "hold spurious writings to be the authentic *Dharma*" and will concoct their own Sutras and falsely claim that the Buddha allows the eating of meat, whereas He says—He does not.

A long passage in the *Lankavatara Sutra* shows the Buddha speaking out very forcefully against meat consumption and unequivocally in favour of vegetarianism, since the eating of the flesh of fellow sentient beings is said by Him to be incompatible with the compassion that a *Bodhisattva* should strive to cultivate.[21]

It is a mystery to me that after such a harsh denunciation of non-vegetarianism, why is it so widespread in the Buddhist world. Probably, the Buddhist's especially Mahayana's need to contemplate a bit deeper if eating meat is in sync with their mission of achieving *Bodhicitta*—a state of mind that desires well-being of all sentient beings.

H.H. Dalai Lama came very close to such a realization. Once as He was travelling, He saw apathy of some life stock who were destined to be killed for food. He got so overwhelmed that He decided to turn vegetarian. Though this vegetarianism did not last long, yet He did receive a right insight.

Similarly, Urgyen Trinley Dorje, strongly urged vegetarianism upon his students, saying that generally, in his view, it was very important in the Mahayana not to eat meat and that even in Vajrayana students should not eat meat. He says:

> There are many great masters and very great realized beings in India and there have been many great realized beings in Tibet also, but they are not saying, "I'm realized, therefore I can do anything; I can eat meat and drink alcohol." It's nothing like that. It should not be like that. According to the Kagyupa school, we have to see what the great masters of the past, the past lamas of Kagyupas, did and said about eating meat. The Drinking Shakpa [sp?] Rinpoche, master of Drikungpa, said like this, "My students, whomever are eating or using meat and calling it tsokhor or "tsok (A Tantric tradition), then these people are completely deserting me and going against the dharma." I can't explain each of these things, but he said that anybody that is using meat and saying it is something good, this is completely against the dharma and against me and they completely have nothing to do with dharma. He said it very, very strongly.[23]

Thus, as far as Shraman tradition is concerned, vegetarianism is the essence of it—both in its Jain and Buddhist versions and any deviation from this central trait is a corruption of the message of the enlightened ones.

Discussion

- Your theory of Christ having lived with Tibetan lamas is completely fraudulent. It was an invention of Notovitch to claim some cheap publicity. The lamas of Hemis have also affirmed that they do not have any *Sutras* which Notovitch claimed to have seen there. Thus, it's not good to mention fraudulent theories to bring forward your point! Please explain.

- If Jesus had an India connection and if the source of His knowledge were Shramans (both Jains and Buddhists as the Manuscript at Hemis claims) then there should have been some reference to this fact by Jesus Himself. Why does there exist no such mention?

Question

Your theory of Christ having lived with Tibetan Lamas is completely fraudulent. It was an invention of Notovitch to claim some cheap publicity. The lamas of Hemis have also affirmed that they do not have any Sutras which Notovitch claimed to have seen there. Thus, it's not good to mention fraudulent theories to bring forward your point! Please explain.

It's correct that lamas of Hemis denounced existence of *Sutras* which Notovitch claimed to have seen. But did we make any efforts to verify this claim of lamas? Maybe they are lying in order to assure a greater cause—the liberation of Tibet. They know to achieve it they will need support of Western countries which are prominently Christian. And thus they fear being alienated by them on accepting Tibetan roots of Jesus!

I may be grossly wrong in the above analysis, but there is really much more in the claims of Notovitch of Jesus having spent His missing years in India. Let's try and discover the same by first reading the *Sutras* which Notovitch claimed to have seen. The *Sutra* is as under:

"A divine infant is born in far-away Israel, and is given the name Issa (Jesus). Sometime during the fourteenth year of his life, the lad arrives in the region of the Sindh (the Indus) in the company of merchants, 'and he settled among the Aryans, in the land beloved of God, with the intention of perfecting himself and of learning from the laws of the great Buddha'. The young Issa travels through the land of five rivers (the Punjab), stays briefly

with '*erring Jains*', and then proceeds to Jagannath where the white priest of Brahma honored him with a joyous reception. At Jagannath Issa/Jesus learns to read and understand the Veda."³⁷

The *Sutra* further claims that Jesus soon developed differences with the priests at Jagannath and then travelled to Tibet to learn Buddhism.

It is this above *Sutra* that is the source of the claim that Christ had an India connection. The Church denounces it as a publicity gimmick of some India centric person.

How correct is this claim. Was Notovitch a fraud? The answer in most likelihood is—no.

I say this not because I am an Indian, and my ego gets pumped up by this fact, but because there is another deep clue in the above description of Notovitch that proves that this manuscript has to be true and is not an invention of Notovitch to gain cheap publicity. This clue has till date escaped the eyes of the world.

This clue is the reference of Jains as "erring". Only a Buddhist could write it. Because since the dawn of Buddhism, they have been referring to Jains as "erring"!

If they would have written this manuscript, if it actually did exist, and if Jesus actually came to India and spent a few of his early days with Jains, then only a Buddhist could write this incident as "stays briefly with erring Jains". This phrase can not be an invention of Notovitch. Also worth considering is the fact that Buddhist annals, as described by Notovitch does not refer to Hindu Brahmins and Vedas as erroneous. This is in spite of the fact that the Brahmin religion and teachings of *Vedas* are totally opposite to that of Buddha!

Only a Buddhist mind could have thought off this way. Since Jainism was in direct competition with Buddhism, so only a Buddhist thought could have considered it worthy of maligning Jains so a higher platform could be achieved by their sect in Shraman Tradition. Only a Buddhist mind could have referred to Jains as "erring".

Such a terminology and writing cannot be an invention of a European who would have no inherent rivalry with Jains. It can only come from the pen of a Buddhist, who just wrote down his mind, without even a slightest thought.

My attempt is not to criticize the writer of the above manuscript. I apologize, if I did that, but I am just trying to bring out my point of view, and trying to point out the fact that there is a deep truth behind spotting of the above Buddhist manuscript about Jesus by Notovitch, and that this issue deserves more research.

There is another clue that I would want to point out. The manuscript above claims that when Jesus arrived in India His first adobe was with Jain monks. Now what could be the reason of this? Why Jains? Jains had never been a very large community in India. Their proportion in the Indian populace had always remained less than approximately 1%! In this land, where majority of the people were Hindus or Buddhists, why did Jesus choose a sect that was in the least proportion? Was it just a coincidence? Or was there a reason of it?

Whenever one travels overseas, he normally has a set destination where he goes and settles. Did Jesus have Jains as a predefined destination to seek shelter on his great journey for spiritual quest to India? And if so, then did there exist someone in the Palestine and the neighbouring region, to which Jesus would have been associated with who could have referred Him to go to Jain monks in India?

The answer in most likelihood is—yes.

Two centuries before Christ, a remarkable mystical movement arose among Jews of Alexandria of Egypt and Palestine. In Egypt, these mystics were known as Therapeutae. Their spiritual brethren in Palestine called themselves Essence and Nazarenes.[37] Their lifestyle and philosophy was very similar to that of Jains, and totally different to the general way of life of the Mediterranean region.

These mystical movements have long baffled historians and the sharp contrast of their lifestyle from mainstream Jews and their proximity to Shraman Theology in India has been a topic of intense contemplation.

For example, unlike the majority of Jews, they stayed away from the bloody ritual performed at the temple of Jerusalem, renounced their properties and lived an ascetic lifestyle, followed celibacy and were strictly vegetarian.[37] This at first sight looks an exact parallel to the lifestyle of Shraman monks and nuns in India.

In most liklihood, Jesus was a part of this mystical movement. So was John the Baptist, who initiated Jesus into their spiritual movement.[38]

If these monks were in some way connected to Jains in India, then it can well be established easily that Jesus could have been referred to some Jain sect during His voyage to India.

I did some research on the similarities between these two movements and take pleasure to discuss the same. The base of this research is the writings of Philo, a distinguished writer at the time of Jesus.

To start with, the most important similarity between these two traditions is a realization that desires are endless. The Therapeutae called desires—"most insatiable of all beasts!"

This declaration is very close to Shraman Theology as it's considered the foundation stone of any further progression on the ladder to Godhood.

Jina says:

Even If One Possesses Uncountable Mountains As High As Mt Kailash of Gold & Silver, Still The Greed is Not Satisfied; Because Desires Are As Endless As Sky.

—*Samansuttam Sutra,* 98

Based on the foundation of this realization, these mysterious ascetics resorted to self-restraint.

As per Philo:

"First of all (they) laid down temperance (self-restraint) as a sort of foundation for the soul to rest upon, (then) proceed to build up other virtues on this foundation."[21]

Temperance is also central to Jain tradition. It's called *Sanyam*—self-restraint and is the foundation on which the entire Shraman Theology rests. It's the point where a being raises above the fourth *Guna* and stations itself at fifth.

As per Jina:

If You Want to Cross Over From This Never Ending Cycle of Repeated Birth's, Then O' Virtuous One, Immediately Board the Ship of Tapas (austerities) & Sanyam (self-restraint).
—*Samansuttam Sutra,* 74

In Shraman tradition, based on the foundations of *Sanyam,* what flowers is the sixth *Guna* and the seeker renounces the material world and becomes a monk or a nun. This is exactly what these seekers of these mysterious movements of the Middle East did.

According to Philo:

"Because of their anxious desire for in immortal and blessed existence, thinking that their mortal life has already come to an end, they leave their possessions to their sons and daughters or perhaps to other relations giving them up their inheritance with willing cheerfulness. . . ."[39]

Having renounced the material world, these seekers; like their Shraman contemporaries in India, lived in simple houses away from the society and dedicated their time and energy to studying scriptures and meditation.

As per Philo:

". . . and they eat nothing of a costly character, but plain bread and a seasoning of salt, which the more luxurious of them to further season with hyssop; and their drink is water from the spring; for they oppose those feelings which nature has made mistresses of the human race, namely, hunger and thirst, giving them nothing to flatter or humor them, but only such useful things as it is not possible to exist without. . . ."

". . . they eat only so far as not to be hungry, and they drink just enough to escape from thirst, avoiding all satiety as an enemy of, and a plotter against both soul & body".[40]

That's the way Shraman's do. This process of feeding the body with just the minimal required food for it to survive is called *Anodri*. It's one of the *Tapas* (austerity) performed by Shraman's daily.

As per Jina:

Ascetics Should Not Take Food for the Sake of Physical Strength, Taste, Bodily Improvements or Luster; They Just Eat Enough to be Able to Achieve The Perfect Knowledge, Sanyam (Self-Control) and Meditation.

—*Samansuttam Sutra,* 406

The above description of Therapeutae, also bring out another similarity between the two traditions. It's the belief in duality of body and soul. Mark the above words—"plotter against both body and soul".

This means that they believed in duality of body and soul. This is very central to Jain tradition. It's the point, where this mysterious movement takes a course, different from Buddhism (as Buddhism do not believe in existence of soul) and becomes more close to Jainism, because belief in existence of soul (*Jiva*) is the crux of Jain ideology. Furthermore, like Jain's in India, they were used to performing long fasts. Philo says:

> "... *and some men, in whom there is implemented a more reverent desire of knowledge, can endure to cherish a recollection of their food for three days without even tasting it. And some men are so delighted, and enjoy themselves so exceedingly when regaled by wisdom... that they can even hold out twice as great a length of time, and would scarcely at the end of six days taste even necessary food....*"[40]

The above passage clearly indicates the most important austerity *(Tapas)* of Jains, viz. *Anshan* (long fasts) being carried out in the Middle East. And what's more important is the fact that it was carried out not for the sake of any extra terrestrial or any after life benefits, but for the sake of knowledge and wisdom.

This is exactly how Jina proposed these fasts to be carried out in Shraman tradition. As per Jina:

> *The One Who Fasts For The Sake Of Attaining Knowledge Through Study, Has Been Referred to As Tapasvi (one practicing penance) in the Agam's (Holy Scriptures). Fasting Without Resorting to Study Amounts Only to Starving.*
> —*Samansuttam Sutra,* 446

Furthermore, in the line of these similarities, both these traditions were divided into monks and nuns. In Shraman tradition, they are called *Sadhu* and *Sadhavi*. In the Middle East, they were called Therapeutae (male monks) and Therapeutrides (female nuns).

According to Philo,

"Now the lifestyle of these philosophers is at once displayed from the appellation given to them; for strict regard to etymology, they are called Therapeutae & Therapeutrides".[39]

Another amazing similarity is that both traditions resorted to truth as the core of the entire spiritual elevation.
As per Philo in the Therapeutae:

"For in short they practice entire simplicity, looking upon falsehood as the foundation of pride, but truth as the origin of simplicity, and upon truth and falsehood as standing in the light of fountains, for from falsehood proceed every variety of evil and wickedness. And from truth there flows every imaginable abundance of good things, both human and divine."[40]

The above belief is central to Shraman philosophy. Compare the above with the below *Sutras* of Jina:

"Just as Ocean is the Adobe of all Fishes, Similarly Truth is the Adobe of Tapas (austerities), Sanyam (self-control) and all Other Virtues."
—Samansuttam Sutra, 96

Comparison between the two cannot be ignored. Compare another similarity as under:
According to Philo, Therapeutae did not consume wine or ate costly seasonings. As per him they believed:

"Wine is the medicine of folly and costly seasoning and sauces excite desire, which is the most insatiable of all beasts."[39]

As per Jina, the above statement is the characteristic of a *Samyag Drishti* being (one who has right vision of leading life). He says:

> *The One Has Been Transformed by Samyag Darshan (Right Vision) Renounces Eating of Five Udamber Fruits and Seven Vices (one of them being wine).*
>
> —*Samansuttam Sutra,* 302

Furthermore, like the Shraman's in India, these mysterious movements believed in equality of all living creatures. At least all human beings! For this reason, they were the first people in that part of the world to have voluntarily given up all slaves as they considered slavery as inhuman. In fact, they were so deep in the belief of equality of all humans that they did not even keep servants. As per Philo:

> *"... and they did not use the ministration of slaves, looking upon the possession of servants or slaves to be a thing absolutely and wholly contrary to nature, for nature has created all men free...."*[39]

The above is also perfectly in tune with Shraman believes and values system. As per Jina:

> *The One Whom You Want to Exploit is Same as You; The One Whom You Want to Administer is Also Same as You.*
> —Ibid., 152
>
> *Just as You Do Not Like Dukha (grief), Same way No One Likes it Either. Knowing This Principle, Treat Others With Respect & Compassion.*
> —Ibid., 150

The above description of these mysterious sects of Middle East makes them an exact parallel of their counterparts in India. They were certainly men and women of highest virtues. They certainly were Shramans of that land. I bow down to them with utmost respect.

However, this similarity between the two traditions does not end here. They are still many more parallels to be discovered that can further strengthen the claim that both the traditions had a similar root. One of such exceptionally startling similarity is the importance of the Fiftieth Day in both the traditions.

Fiftieth day was very auspicious to these mysterious movements of the Middle East. According to Philo:

> "In the first place, these men assemble at the end of the seven weeks . . . which is assigned to the number fifty . . . which is the principle of the origination and condition of the whole."

Fiftieth day in Shraman Theology also has a great reverence. According to Shraman Theology, as the current *Kala-Chakra* (cosmic wheel of time) started, the first twenty-one thousand years at Earth were like a living hell. It was a rocky and barren planet which was too hot to make any civilization possible. However, humanity still existed and lived in caves and ventured out early in the morning or late in the nights for hunting food. But at the end of these twenty-one thousand years, there were heavy rains which lasted for seven weeks. At the end of these rains, the Earth turned around completely and it was green and pleasant everywhere.

It was on this day the humans left the caves forever and formed civilized societies. Thus, this fiftieth day has a great reverence in Shraman tradition and their most auspicious festival—*Samvatsari* is still celebrated on the fiftieth day of start of rainy season to mark that day. It's the oldest festival of our planet, the first we humans ever celebrated.

The above description of Philo of these mysterious Mediterranean movements seems to indicate a similar belief in the origination of human civilization. Mark the words "principle of origination and condition of the whole". It seems they have been deriving their believes from a similar knowledge bank as Jains in India.

Another similarity, which is almost impossible to ignore between the two traditions is the way they performed their prayers. As per Philo, these mysterious movements:

> "... are accustomed to pray twice a day, at morning and at evening; when sun is rising and when the sun is setting.... They pray that their souls, being entirely lightened and relieved of the burden of outward senses...."[39]

This is exactly how the Shraman's perform their most important prayer—*Pratikarman*. It's performed twice a day, at the time of sun rises and sun sets. And the purpose of this prayer is the same as that was of these mysterious movements—to lighten the burden of *Karmas* accumulated on the soul.

Taking forward these similarities between the two traditions is the similar structure of their church. In these ascetic movements of Middle East, Philo says:

> "They do not look on those as elders who are advanced in years and very ancient, but in some cases they esteem those as very young men if they have attached themselves to the sect only lately; but those whom they call elders are those who from their earliest infancy have grown up and arrived at maturity in the speculative portion of philosophy...."[39]

That's exactly how Shraman churches are organized. The elder of the Shraman is not the one who is oldest of the group, but the one who has longest life as an ascetic.

Furthermore, there is another surprising similarity between their churches. This similarity is in their common religious place. As per Philo:

"The common place where they all come together on the seventh day is a two-fold circuit, being separated partly into the apartment of men, and partly into the chamber of women . . . and the wall which is in between the houses rises from ground three or four cubits upwards. . . ."[39]

". . . and the order to which thy sit down to meet is a divided one, the men sitting on the right hand and women apart from them on the left; . . . (on) rugs of the coarest material, cheap mats of the most ordinary kind of papyrus of the land, piled up on ground. . . ."[39]

This description resemble the description of common religious place of Swetambera Jain. Its called—*Sthanak*. They are the common place where all lay followers of Shraman traditions called—*Shravak* and *Shravika* flock in, to listen discourses of the monks and nuns. These *Sthanaks* like the common places of the Mediterranean sects are divided into two sections each for men and women, divided by a small wooden wall. Men sit on cheap mats on laid on the ground on the right hand side of the *Sthanak* and women on the left.

The similarities just seem to be endless and seem to keep getting more and more profound. In continuation of the same, comes the next.

Philo, while describing their celebrations on the fiftieth day says:

"Therefore, when they come together clothed in white garments, and joyful with most exceeding gravity, when someone of the ephemereutae (one's participating in the celebrations), before they sit down to meet, standing in order in a row, and raising their eyes and their heads to heaven . . . they pray to God. . . ."

"They all stand up together, and in the middle of entertainment two choruses are formed at first, the one of men and other of women, and each chorus there is a leader and chief selected, who is the most honorable of the band. Then they sing hymn's which have been composed in honor of God in many meters and tunes, at the

time of sitting together and at another moving their hands and dancing in corresponding harmony, and uttering an inspired manner, songs of thanksgiving, at another time regular odes, and performing all necessary strophes and antistrophes."[39]

This is too great a similarity to be just a coincidence. This seems to be description of annual *Samvatsari Pratikarman* being performed by lay Shraman followers. Because this is exactly how they do it till today! On the fiftieth day of start of rainy season, to celebrate *Samvatsari*, the lay followers gather together, clad in white clothes. They form two groups, one of men (*Shravak*) and another of women (*Shravika*). The most learned among them becomes the group leader and chairs the entire program. The above description of Philo is an exact representation of what happens in the process.

The above similarities between Jains in India and the mysterious similar movements in the Middle East are too hard to ignore. These cannot just be coincidence. There had to be a connection between the two.

It's possible that Shraman Theology, either after the time of Jina, or may be even before the time of Jina (as He was only the last of the Twenty-Four Great Masters of this tradition) could have spread its wings outside the Indian subcontinent. India in those days commanded a lion's share of world economy and was very well connected to the rest of the world.

Ports of Gujarat those days were major trading centers between India and the Middle East. And Swetambera Jain community is till date one of the most influential trading communities of the region. It's possible that some traders of the Mediterranean region, having inspired by their Indian Jain counterparts, could have carried their philosophy back to their country and sowed the seeds of rise of these mysterious movements. It's also possible that Indian traders venturing into the Middle East could have done so.

Another theory that may be considered is the historically

proven fact that when Alexander was on his way back after his mayhem in the North Western part of India (today's Pakistan), he wanted to take back Indian Theology. He was a disciple of the legendary Aristotle, and had instructions of bringing back art and literature of the conquered territories along with their philosophy and ideas.

There is every possibility that he could have carried this Jain philosophy back to Macedonia and his new cultural and spiritual center at the mouth of Nile—the city of Alexandria. He invaded India in the year 325 B.C.

Therapeutae and Essenes movements arose to become noteworthy in that region in another 100 years after that, which is a reasonable amount of time for any new religion or idea to become popular.

There is every possibility that this Jain philosophy which the Greek army brought back home, could have acted as seeds of these mysterious Mediterranean sects. But since there was no real contact with the mainstream Jainism in India, these sects then grew on their own, adapting the basic Jain ideas and mixing them with their own ideas and believes of the beyond.

More clues that point to the above mysterious movements to have a foreign source is the fact that as per Philo, they possessed "some arcane (secret) writings of their own tradition".[21] He says:

"They have also writings of ancient men, who having been founders of one sect or another have left behind them many memorials of the allegorical system of writings and explanations, whom they take as a kind of model. . . ."[40]

The above description means that these writings were different from the ones like *The Old Testament* and other books which normal Jews referred to. These secret books could be based on the seeds of Shraman Theology which the traders or invading Greek armies carried with themselves to the Middle East.

The astonishing similarities that we just discussed above could be a result of these mysterious movements deriving their knowledge from these secret writings

Thus, it can well be established that the above mysterious movements had a foreign connection and that connection was the Swetambera Jain Shraman tradition in India. Thus, when one of their sons, Jesus embarked on a spiritual quest to seek knowledge, He would have been told to seek out for Jain monks when He reached India. This explains why He preferred to stay with Jains, which was almost an insignificant tradition when He arrived in India.

But what if this was not the case? What if the above theory of Therapeutae, Essence and Nazarenes being an extension of Shramans in India could not be proofed historically?

Even then I have reasons to believe that Jesus would have chosen Jains as His first adobe in India. The reason is that He would have been equally astonished to find wandering Indian Swetambara Jain monks following a similar lifestyle and believes like those of the mysterious Jew sects of His homeland.

This surprisingly similar sect of ascetics would have increased His curiosity to know more about them and thus He would have joined them and stayed with them on His visit to India.

Thus, the reference of Jesus staying with Jains cannot be just an invention of Notovitch. There is a far deeper truth in this statement. If he was to invent this manuscript on his own, he would not have bothered to write that Jesus stayed briefly with Jains and not specifically referred to them as "erring".

On the contrary, he would have written that Jesus stayed with Hindus. Or he would have written that Jesus stayed at a Buddhist monastery. As these two religions were the most popular religions of the time.

But this is not the case. Thus, this mention of Jain and an

addition of an adjective of "erroneous" to them is in itself a proof that Notovitch could not have invented this manuscript, and that he actually referred to a historical piece of literature.

This declaration of Notovitch deserves deeper research. His hard work cannot be permitted to go down the drain, or otherwise, the world will be ripped of one of the most important historical facts of human civilization. I request my Buddhist brothers to help in solving this mystery, because they are the treasurers of this global heritage and the truth about the unknown life of Jesus—The Christ

Question

If Jesus had an India connection and if the source of His knowledge were Shramans (both Jains and Buddhists as the Manuscript at Hemis claims) then there should have been some reference to this fact by Jesus Himself? Why does there exist no such mention?

There does exist a very deep connection. We discussed the similarity between the Christian Trinity of The Father, The Son and The Holy Spirit and the Shraman fundamentals of The Siddha, The Buddha and The Dharma earlier in this discussion. It can not just be a coincidence.

Furthermore, there is a remarkable similarity between the teachings of the two traditions, at least at the starting level. The below *Sutras* of Jina and Jesus prove the same:

What You Desire For Yourself, Desire for Others Too, What You Do Not Desire For Yourself, Do Not Desire For Others Too, This Is The Message Of The Jina—The Enlightened One.
—*Jina (Samansuttam Sutra, 24)*

So in everything, do to others what you would have them do to you, for this sums up the Law and the Prophets.
—*Jesus (Matthew 7:12)*

The similarity is not hard to pinpoint. And these similarities have long astonished the ones who are aware of both traditions. A researcher Rudolf Seydel, a German philosopher and theologian has noted around fifty such similarities between Shraman and Christian teachings.

Keveli—The State of Godhood

9

Keveli—The State of Godhood

One, Whose All Delusive Karmas Are Annihilated And Whose Mind Is Clean Like Water Placed In A Crystal Made Vessel has been called by the enlightened Master as Kshin Moh Nirgranth Monk.
—*Samansuttam Sutra*, 561

FINALLY, THE journey ends. The seeker claims his Godhood.

12. *Transcendence of Mind (Kshin Moh),* (13) *State of the Supreme Soul with Body (Sahyogi Keveli Jin),* (14) *State of Moksha or Nirvana (Ayogi Keveli Jin)*

What happens after the last battle? A seeker transcends his last mind. The last and the most subtle layer of mind also fall, and the seeker attains enlightenment. This is the last stage. There are still two more stages to go, but still it's termed as the last stage, because now onwards, there is nothing left for the seeker to do. This is the point of no return. The seeker cannot fall back into the mundane states from this point onwards. At this point, he has conquered his mind in entirety and has thus destroyed all the impurities of mind like greed, lust, passions, attachments and desires. Such a person is like a lake whose water has become totally pure. Now there is no dirt left over at its bottom either, so even if there is movement in this lake, still no dirt will come on top, because there is no dirt leftover in it.

There is a story from the life of Buddha. Once a person

came to him and spat at his face. Imagine ourselves in such a situation. What will happen? We will immediately react. Our anger will burst over like a volcano. The same probably will be the case in a seeker at eleventh stage. Whatsoever heights he may have achieved in his spiritual growth, howsoever clean and pure he may appear, but if he still has any ego leftover, in any sublime form, at the bottom of his mind, its bound to come up.

Like dirt at the bottom of a lake in mountain comes up with any movement in lake. Similarly, a movement has been made in the mind of a pure looking seeker. If there is any dirt of mind, the same will get back on top. But Buddha remained unmoved. There was no reaction to this action on him. He had already crossed the eleventh stage. The *Sutra* that describes this state of a seeker says as follows:

One, Whose All Delusive Karmas Are Annihilated And Whose Mind Is Clean Like Water Placed In A Crystal Made Vessel has been called by the enlightened Master as Kshin Moh Nirgranth Monk.
—Samansuttam Sutra, 561

A monk, whose mind is as clean as water kept in a crystal vessel. The *Sutra* uses very apt descriptive words. It says that the mind is not just clean like clean water, but as clean as clean water kept in a crystal vessel. Why? Why has this *Sutra* used the word crystal vessel? Perhaps this is done to explain the height of purity of the mind of a seeker at this stage. If a vessel has any impurities, then the same can be reflected back from the clean water. So the *Sutra* says as clean as the clean water placed in a crystal vessel! At this stage, there are no impurities leftover to be reflected back. There is no possibility leftover of the rising of any impurities, for any reason or any circumstance.

Another very descriptive word that this *Sutra* uses to describe the state of such a monk is *Nirgranth*. *Nir* means without and *granthi* means knots. So literally this word translates into knotless. Traditionally, this word has been used by Jains to describe a monk who has left all worldly possessions, including clothes and has become nude.

What does this *Sutra* means by *Nirgranth* here? The meaning that the Jain scriptures denote to this word is *Nisang*, which means, detached of all worldly objects and desires. If we take this meaning, then such a seeker could be described as someone, for whom the importance of worldly objects ceases to exist. For him, presence or absence of worldly objects becomes meaningless. If they are present, he is ok with them. There state or condition does not affect him. If they cease to exist, he is still ok without them.

This second meaning is perhaps more apt, in the above *Sutra,* because this is how Jina Himself got nude. He is supposed to have renounced everything, except for a sheet of blanket which was supposed to have been offered to Him by demigods. He did not become nude as a compulsion. This means that He did not consider nudity to be of any importance, while renouncing the material world. But as He moved on, a beggar came to Him for alms. He tore the sheet into two and gave half of the sheet to the beggar.

Consider this situation. He tore the sheet into two, keeping half with himself. Why? Was He attached to the sheet? Is this an indication of slight attachment towards His only left worldly possession—a divine sheet of cloth! Or is Jina actually trying not to get nude?

No, according to me it's none of the above. It's a simple state of mind of a *Nisang* Monk. A monk for whom the importance of attachments has ceased to exist! So, whether the sheet of cloth is full or half does not make any difference. And He moved on, with the half piece of cloth covering His body. And then, that sheet got entangled in thorns of a bush. And He again moved on, leaving that half sheet of cloth as well, totally naked. He did not consider that half piece of cloth also worthy enough to make an effort to free it from thorns. Such is a state of mind of someone, who has attained a state of *Nisang mind*. And this is perhaps, what this *Sutra* means while describing a monk as *Nirgranth*. Someone totally detached!

Whenever Buddha referred to Jina, He referred to Him as *Nigantha (Nirgrantha) Nattaputta*. *Nigantha (Nirgrantha)* means knotless or one who has broken free from all bonds and *Nataputta* means the son of the Natta clan. So Jina was referred to by Buddha as a son of the Natta family who has broken free from all bonds that tie a person down to this world. This further explains that the word *nirgranth* means more of detached. Nudity may arise out of this state of mind, as it took place in Jina but it does not mean naked.

Having thus discovered His Godhood, the seeker now enter into the Thirteenth ladder—*State of the Supreme Soul with Body (Sahyogi Keveli Jin)* and remains in this state till the *Ayushya Karma* (the age deciding actions of past life) and the balance three *Non-Harming (Agathiya) Karmas* we discussed earlier completely gets annihilated. Till this annihilation takes place, the seeker remains at this thirteenth *Guna* and is referred to as—*Arihant* (in Buddhism they are called *Arhats*). This is a state of God in material body and their presence becomes a bacon of light for the rest of humanity.

Amid these *Arihant's*, as per Shraman Theology, our planet happens to experience Forty-eight special illustrious *Arihants* in its each *Kala-Chakra* (the wheel of time) who become responsible of spreading the Shraman Theology on our planet. Amid these Forty-eight, the first Twenty-four appear when our planet is on an upward cycle of *Kala-Chakra* and the last Twenty-four appear when our planet is on a downward phase of *Kala-Chakra*. These Forty-eight special *Arihant's* are called—*Tirthankars*. *Jina*—*The Mahavira*—who imparted us the knowledge of these Fourteen *Gunas*, and the source of all the *Sutras* we discussed above and the ones we will discuss in the proceeding volumes of this discussion was the last of these Forty-eight *Tirthankars* on our planet.

The balance numerous seekers who achieves this state, and will achieve them in times to come are simply referred to as—*Keveli*. At base, both *Tirthankar's* and *Kevelis* are same. *Tirthankars* in spite of being special *Kevelis* are not considered superior to *Kevelis*. They both, together are referred to as—*Arihants* (Buddhist—*Arhats*) and are the ones whom the Shraman pay their first homage in the *Namokar Mantra*—their greatest *Sutra*.

As the four *Non-Harming (Agathiya) Karmas* of these *Arihants* come to an end, they leave their material body and enter the Fourteenth *Guna* and become *Ayogi Keveli Jin*. *Ayogi* means someone whose bond between the material body and soul gets annihilated.

This is the last step of an association of a liberated being with this *Samsara*—the material world. Within moments of having achieved this state, the soul merges into the soul of previous enlightened masters called *Siddha* and becomes one with them. This state is referred to as *Moksha* or *Nirvana*. It's perhaps this stage which Jesus described as—reunion with the Father. The soul of the seeker unites with the soul of the previous liberated beings and the two becomes one.

Moksha, Sanskrit *Moksha* ("release"), also called *Mukti*, or *Apavarga*, in Indian religions, is the ultimate spiritual goal, designating the individual soul's release from the bonds trapped in a chain of successive rebirths (*Samsara*) until it has reached perfection or the enlightenment that allow its release, or *Moksha*.[3]

Here, the Enlightened Master leaves the body, forever and liberates himself from the cycle of birth and death. We have called such masters *Jin* meaning victorious. One who has won the battle over mind and its desires and passions! One who has won the battle over death, forever!

There are many paths, and doctrines available in oriental

religions to attain this highest stage of humanity, but no one till now perhaps did such a detailed step by step analyses of the stages that lead to Godhood as the stages described in the above Shraman *Sutras.*

After reading about the *Sutras,* a desire is bound to arise in us to transcend all of them quickly. We may want to jump over all of them as soon as possible and want to experience the ultimate. Say, for example, if we analyze ourselves and find ourselves at the fourth stage of *Conscious Uncontrolled (Avirata SamyagDrishti)*, then we would immediately want to set ourselves in borders and jump to the fifth stage of *Defining one's boundaries (Desh Virakt)* and so on. If such is a case, then as far as I have understood The Jina, we will be committing a great blunder.

The above stages are not something we can achieve by adapting ourselves to look like the seeker on that stage. These are more of a happening than doing. To understand it better, let's get to the very beginning of the *Sutra* we had been contemplating above. The very onset of this *Sutra* says:

> *Those States Resulting From the Fruitation etc. of Karmas (Actions), By Which Souls Are Distinguished, are Given Name "GUNA" (spiritual stages) By The Omniscient.*

The above stages are achieved as fruition. What is the meaning of fruition? Is fruition an action? Or is it a happening If we evaluate deeply, we will come to a conclusion that fruition is a happening. It's an end-result of the combination of all the ingredients that are required for it to happen. It cannot be forced upon. It happens. We cannot put all the ingredients together and force the fruit to appear. It will happen on its own accord when the time is ripe. The same is the case of the above stages. They cannot be achieved by forcing ourselves into accepting the requirements of a particular stage.

Say, for example, if someone wants to uplift himself from fourth to fifth, then he may start acting like a seeker on the fifth stage. He may force himself into turning vegetarian. But if this turning is superficial and not out of compassion and love for forms of life that are lower than his, then probably it will not have any effect on him. Then this stage will fail to become a stepping stone for him to elevate any further.

On the contrary, if a seeker at the fourth stage instead of forcing himself into accepting a vegetarian way of life, understand the message of the enlightened master, and agrees to the fact that all forms of life have an equal right to exist, then he would automatically resort to *Ahimsa* (non-violent way of life) which in turn will make him vegetarian. This turning into a vegetarian will happen as a result of fruition of his turning non-violent at heart and will uplift him to the fifth stage.

Before we proceed any further, it is important to consider another aspect of the *Sutras* we are contemplating on. Legends have it that they were never spoken of. They were just heard of in silence by the intimate ones sitting by the side of The Jina. It is one of the most miraculous things. There was an inner circle of eleven intimate disciples around Jina who simultaneous heard these *Sutras* within themselves. Jina did not say a word, but in a deep silence all the eleven disciples heard them simultaneously. Please emphasize on the word simultaneously. And when they all heard the same words, they thought it worth while to record them. And that's how these *Sutras* were born. And this is what makes these *Sutras* special. One cannot conceive of a more beautiful beginning, and they certainly contain the highest light man is capable of, and the whole science of conquering oneself.[15]

These *Sutras* were then transmitted orally generation after generation. About 200 years after the *Nirvana* of Jina, a terrible feminine broke in Northern India. At that time the monk named Sthulabhadra was in charge *(Acharya)* of the Jains in North and was the last man who knew all these *Sutras* collectively referred to as the Fourteen *Purvas*. Fearing the loss of this sacred knowledge on account of this never before witnessed feminine, he convoked a council at Patliputra (today's Patna) in which the first Ten *Purvas* were rearranged in Twelve *Angas*. The last four were not documented as they were forbidden to be thought to general populace on account of some special knowledge vested in them. Subsequently, the last Four *Purvas* were lost completely.

But why are we discussing this? First, to thank this legendary sage, who took this bold decision to document these *Sutras*! It's his courtesy that we have them today, and are contemplating over them, hoping to help them churn our own life forces, and push us towards the supreme goal of Moksha. Had the conclave not been called by him, these *Sutras* would also have been lost like the last Four *Purvas*.

Second reason to discussing this fact, is to remember that, the *Sutras*, were probably not conveyed in the same chronology as we are discuss them. In fact, the current form of *Samansuttam*, the holy Jain book that is being used as a source of these *Sutras*, was conceived only in the early Twentieth Century by the efforts of one of the greatest Hindu Mystic of his times, Sri Acharaya Vinoba. Until then, the *Sutras*, though preserved in their original form, were divided into different Jain books, called *Agams*. The current chronology, as set in *The Saman Suttam*, was set up only 2500 years after they originally came into existence. So the *Sutras* we will discuss first are not necessarily the prior *Sutras* and the *Sutras* we will discuss later will not necessarily be later *Sutras* required on spiritual elevation of a seeker. Understanding all the *Sutras* as one unit will only revel to us their true meaning!

DISCUSSION

- What is *Kala-Chakra*?
- If we wish to tread this path to Godhood and join the

Shraman religion, which of its two traditions—the Buddhism or Jainism you recommend?
- What's the logic behind the force of *Dharma* and *Adharma*? And for that matter in all the six *Dravyas* (elementary substances) of Shraman Theology?

Question
What is Kala-Chakra?

Kala-Chakra, as the name symbolizes means wheel of time. As per this theory, our universe does not have any beginning as advocated by modern science nor will it ever end. This claim is one of the most controversial claims of Shraman Theology as it does not seem to be in tune with the findings of modern science.

As per the this theory, just as moon revolves around Earth, and planets revolve around sun, and stars revolve around the black holes, similarly; our universe, with all its galaxies revolve around a super massive celestial structures called *parvat*. This term means mountain and perhaps just as mountains are the greatest structures on our planet, similarly these celestial *Parvats* (mountains) are the greatest structure that exists in our universe. And their sheer size gives them the gravity that makes them move the galaxies around themselves just the same way as black hole makes stars to move around and the stars makes planets to revolve.

Our planet along with our galaxy also orbits this *Parvat*. And the time it takes to complete one orbit is referred to as *Kala-Chakra*.

This analysis of *Kala-Chakra* is based on my understanding of *Sutra*s about our universe in Jain scriptures. These scriptures are one of the most esoteric knowledge of Shraman tradition and in past only those seekers were allowed to read them, who had crossed a minimum of twenty years of ascetic life. If conditions permit, we will discuss these scriptures in future volumes of this book.

This *Kala-Chakra* is divided into two equal halves called *Utsarpani* (progressive) and *Avsarpani* (regressive) with six epochs each (referred to as *Ara*). Each epoch is distinct in itself and leads to change in ecology of our planet. And as one *Kala-Chakra* completes and leads to start of another, the epochs keep repeating themselves. It's just like seasons change as our planet completes its orbit around sun, the same way epochs change as it completes its orbit around the *Parvat*.

These changes in epochs are so massive that at one extreme it makes our planet a living hell and at the other, it makes it a paradise that as per its description in Jain Theology seems to resemble exactly like the description of Garden of Eden in *Bible*. Below figure is a representation of this *Kala-Chakra*.

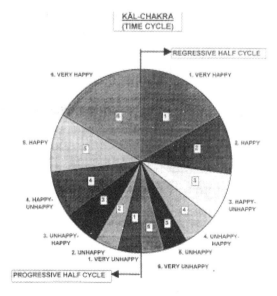

Logically, this model of revolving universe makes complete sense. Knowing the fact that every thing in this universe revolves around something else, it's not hard to believe that the same will be the case of our galaxies too. Still the hard fact is that the scientific facts seem to point otherwise.

The major areas where this theory confronts science are two. The first on the scientific belief of the creation of this universe, i.e. the theory of big bang and second on the principle of its ever-expanding nature!

Now this brings us to a major road block. If the above theory of *Kala-Chakra* is wrong, then it shakes the Shraman Theology at the very roots. A question arises that if it's proved wrong on one front, then there is every possibility that its claims of *Moksha* and *Nirvana* and the formulae of *Tatvas* and its evaluation of release from *Karmas* by following techniques of *Samvar* and *Nirjara* may also be wrong! How can we believe a theology or philosophy that is proved inherently wrong in one of its most fundamental believes? Thus, either this theory of *Kala-Chakra* is wrong, or there is a mistake in interpretation of science in seeing what's happening out there.

This led me to perform a brief research over this subject. I take pleasure to share it with you. Let's start with the first contradiction—The Theory of Big Bang.

I discovered that this theory is not scientifically proved as yet. It's just the most popular speculation as to how it all started. But still it remains a speculation and not a scientific fact. Thus, denouncing the theory of *Kala-Chakra* just because it stands against the theory of Big-Bang will be grossly wrong.

The second confrontation that this theory faces with modern science is its belief in an ever-expanding universe. This belief is based on some real hard proved evidence and scientific calculations that our galaxies are constantly moving away from each other—and thus our universe is constantly expanding!

These calculations are scientifically proven. It's a proven fact that our galaxies are moving away from each other. So in this case, we cannot say that science has erred when it says so. So either the Shraman Theology erred in this case, or the conclusion that our scientific community has made out of these calculations is erred.

I beg to believe in the second. And there is a reason behind my belief as under:-

The theory of expanding universe started in 1927 when a Belgian astrologer Georges Lemaitre first proposed this model. Since then it kept gaining more ground and was firmly established with scientific calculations performed by Sir Edwin Hubble which proved the fact that galaxies are moving apart.

So it's been just about a hundred odd years we have been observing what's happening out there that proposes expanding universe. And as per backward calculation of the rate of this expansion, the science predicts that this process started about a 13.7 billion years ago.

So this means that out of the total number of years since when this movement of galaxies started, the time frame we have been observing it is just a 100 years.

Now let's do some simple arithmetics. The total amount of time that we have been observing it comes out to be 100/13.7 billion years, i.e. 0.00000000729927 of its total proposed life. This means that we have seen these movements for only 0.000000729927% of its total life.

A question I would like to raise here is that—is it possible for us to correctly judge what's happening out there by observing it for only such a small fraction of time of its supposed movement?

Imagine some one here on planet Earth, who does not know that our planet moves around the sun trying to judge its movement vis-à-vis other planets by just observing the sky for 0.000000729927% of year, i.e. just 0.23 seconds!

He may because of his exceptionally good observation conclude that the planets are moving away from each other or coming close to each other depending on their orbit, but not knowing the fact that they are moving on their own orbits, there is a very great likelihood that he may misinterpret that these planets are either moving away from each other or are coming closer to each other and may eventually collide.

This perhaps is the mistake our scientists are also making. Their observation and calculations of redshifts are not wrong, but there interpretation of this calculation is. Because these observations may just be indications of movement of galaxies on their own orbits! Not an expansion of the universe.

And may be, sooner or later, the science will discover the same. It has happened a lot of time in the past that science proved something only to disapprove it later based on new observations. I am sure the same is going to be the fate of the theory of the expanding universe too.

Another scientific observation that goes against the belief of ever-expanding universe is the scientific observation that there are a few galaxies that are actually coming closer to each other rather than following the principle of ever expanding and moving apart galaxies. This is the case of our own galaxy and our immediate neighbor Andromeda galaxy. This does not seem logical because if the galaxies have been constantly expanding from last 13.7 billion years, then there does not seem any reason for these two galaxies to be now coming closer to each other. But if we analyze this observation based on the theory of *Kala-Chakra* then it seems perfectly logical as these two galaxies may be moving in opposite directions on their own orbits.

And finally what makes this model of revolving universe more relevant is the very fact that everything that exists out there revolves. From tiny meteoroids to moons to planets to massive stars! They all revolve around something else. Then there is no reason that our galaxies may be following an exception and moving away from each other. It's just our myopic sight that makes us believe that.

Thus, on my own accord, I would like to believe that

science erred on this account and that the message from the enlightened ones of revolving universe is correct. I welcome comments and feedback from our scientists.

Question

If we wish to tread this path to Godhood and join the Shraman religion, which of its two traditions—the Buddhism or Jainism you recommend?

According to me, both are as good as each other. It really does not make a difference on the tradition we choose. What makes the difference is that—we choose and start moving. The emancipation lies in movement. Not in choosing one over the other.

May the Holy Spirit be with us. May we always remain established in the forces of *Dharmastikaye* (*Dharma Dravya*) by untying out knots of *Adharma Dravya*. The Godhood will blossom on its own accord.

Question

What's the logic behind the force of Dharma and Adharma? And for that matter in all the six Dravyas (elementary substances) of Shraman Theology?

As per Shraman Theology, our universe is made up of six elementary substances called *Dravyas*. This concept of *Dravyas*, like the concept of *Kala-Chakra* we discussed above is also one of the most mystical concepts of Shraman Theology as most Jains feel they are not in tune with modern scientific understanding of the universe.

Fortunately, this is not the case. Let's spare a few moments to understand them, and by the time we will complete this analysis, we will be in a better position to decide for ourselves answer to the question raised above on which religion is better for us—Jainism or Buddhism.

As per Jina, this universe is a net result of inter-mixing and inter-play of six substances. All these substances are sovereign in them self, and have existed since eternity. The *Sutra* which describes them is as under:

> *The Omniscient Jina's Has Described the Universe to be Constituted of Six Substances, viz. Dharma (medium of motion), Adharma (medium of rest), Akasha (space), Kala (time), Pudgal (matter) and Jiva (soul).*
> —*Samansuttam Sutra*, 624

> *These Six Substance Co-exist and Accommodate Each Other. Its so since Times Immemorial. But at the Same Time, They do not Leave Their Own Specific Traits.*
> —*Samansuttam Sutra*, 630

Lets discuss on each of them and understand about their existence from a scientific angle.

Pudgal (Matter) *Pudgal* means matter. Any thing that has mass is *Pudgal*. From tiny sub-atomic particles to the mighty planets and stars are all *Pudgal*. The smallest component of *Pudgal* is called *Parmanu*.

Parmanu is the smallest particle the *Pudgal* can be broken into. These *Parmanus* then join together to form various types of matters and break apart when this matter become too massive to sustain itself! It is from this addition and deletion of *Parmanus* that the word *Pudgal* derives it name from. *Pud* in this word means addition or fusion of *Parmanus* and *Gal* means deletion or fission of *Parmanus*. And it is a result of this addition and deletion of *Parmanus* the entire matter came into existence. From the tiny atoms of various elements to every thing else, known or still unknown that this universe is made off. All are a result of this play between *Parmanus*. Today, modern science has found evidence of the truth of this substance *(Dravya)*. The term *Parmanu* referred to in Jain Theology can be compared to the sub-atomic particle—proton. Today scientists know that it is because of addition and deletion of proton's various elements that we know off are formed. A single proton forms the nucleus of a hydrogen atom. Two protons are found in the nucleus of a helium atom. This is how the elements are formed all the way up to the heaviest naturally occurring substance, uranium, which has 92 protons in its nucleus. Today, scientists know that it is possible to make two free protons (Hydrogen nuclei) come together to make the beginnings of a helium nucleus. This requires that the protons be hurled at each other at a very high speed. This process occurs in the sun, but can also be replicated on Earth with lasers, magnets, or in the center of a nuclear bomb. The process is called nuclear fusion and is referred to as *Pud* in the word *Pudgal*.

Today, we also know that elements heavier than iron are unstable. Some of them are very unstable! This means that their nuclei, composed of many positively charged protons, which want to repel from each other, are liable to fall apart at any moment! We call atoms like this radioactive. Uranium, for example, is radioactive. Every second, many of the atoms in a chunk of uranium are falling apart. When this happens, the pieces, which are now new elements (with fewer protons) are less massive in total than the original uranium atoms. This process is called nuclear fission. And is referred to as *Gal* in the word *Pudgal*. This *Pudgal* (matter) is one of the six constitutes of our universe and modern science fully agrees to this claim.

Akasha (Space) *Akasha* means space that consist all the *Pudgal* (matter) and balance four substances that we will discuss ahead which constitute our universe. *Akasha* is the superset of all the balance five *Dravyas* (substances). It provides the space where balance *Dravyas* could exist and play. *Akasha* consists of two parts. These are *Lokākāsha* (universe) and *Alokākāsh* (non-universe). It's in the *Lokākāsha* (universe) part of *Akasha* that all the other five *Dravyas* (substances) coexist. *Alokākāsh* (non-universe) is beyond the *Lokakāsha* and is empty, it has no other substance. Today, scientists have developed maps of our universe. In this map, they have added all the known galaxies. But they do contemplate that there exist a massive emptiness beyond this universe which might include parallel universes like ours.

Shraman Theology completely agrees with this statement. As per this school, this universe which we see is not the only universe that exists. There are seven universes like ours with intelligent human life as it exists on our planet. And together these seven universes constitute a master universe. Then there are eight more such master-universes that exist. Jina referred to each of them by name. And that's not all. These master universes together constitute just one of the three major parts of our super massive universe and are called—*Lokakāsha*.

It's not possible to discuss all these parts and parallel universes in this discussion. But if conditions permit, we will initiate discussion of the same in a separate volume sometime in future.

As of now, let's concentrate our energies to a scientific analysis of the six substances only. And *Akasha* (space) is perfectly in tune with modern science. Its one of their most favored areas of research and development. If they read Jain scriptures, they can have a plenty of clues on where to look for life out there.

Kala (Time) *Kala* means time. It's the instrument, which permits all the balance five *Dravyas* (substances) to undergo changes. It does not cause changes in them. But provides the required instrument where these changes can take place and be measured. It is third of the six substances that constitute our universe. And scientists will be more than happy to accept it. In fact, scientists are so fascinated with this dimension of our existence that they propose that space and time should be understood in relation to each other have thus devised a theory of Space-Time.

Dharma (medium of motion) Now we come to what started this discussion. The force of *Dharma* or *Dharmastikay* as its referred to in Jain scriptures. The question was raised on the logic behind this force. Let's try and decipher the same. And to do that, let's first understand how this *Dravya* (substance) if defined by Jina.

The *Sutra* that describes this constituent of universe is as under:

> *Just As In This World, Water Acts As A Medium Of Motion For The Fishes, Similarly In This Universe, Dharma Acts As A Medium Of Motion For The Jiva & Pudgal (matter) Elements Of This Universe.*
> —Samansuttam Sutra, 632

Jiva is the last constituent of this universe and we will discuss over it later. But for the moment, let's concentrate on the *Pudgal* (matter). Jina says that *Dharma* is that constituent of this universe which helps in movement of *Pudgal*. Until a few decades back, if scientists were told of existence of any such thing they would have ridiculed it and rejected its existence based on reason that they can not see the same.

But all this changed in 1970s, when an astronomer called Vera Rubin was measuring the velocity of stars in other galaxies. She observed that stars at the edges of galaxies moved faster than those at the centre of the galaxies. This observation was against the popular scientific assumption that the stars at edges would move slower than the ones at the centre because of reduced gravity of the black hole. The reason of this strange movement was attributed to the fact that there exists an invisible substance that we cannot see and was termed as "Dark Matter".

It is this dark matter that is supposed to give that additional force required for these stars to reconcile their orbits to the Newton's law of gravity. Or, in other words, it can be said that it's this dark matter that facilitate the faster movement of these stars. This is exactly what Jina says about *Dharma*—the fourth substance that constitutes this universe. It's supposed to provide the medium that permits stars, planets and other forms of matter—to move.

In another *Sutra* on this subject, Jina says:

> *Dharma is Devoid Of the Attributes like Taste, Color, Smell, Sound & Touch. It Pervades The Entire Universe, Is One Piece, Huge And Is At All Points.*
> —Samansuttam Sutra, 631

This is exactly what scientist's today claim about dark matter. They say it's a special type of substance that does not emit light nor scatters light and does not react to any electromagnetic wave. Or, in other words, it does not have any of the properties like taste, color, smell, sound or touch that normal matter is supposed to have. As per Jina's reference about *Dharma*, they claim that this special substance exists across the universe, is huge and is all pervasive. The similarities between Jina's claim about this fourth substance called *Dharma* and modern science claim about dark matter are so startlingly huge that there is every reason to believe that this astonishing new discovery of science is same as what Jina referred to as *Dharma*—one of the six constituents of this universe.

A question that arises here is why did Jina referred to this substance as *Dharma*? This word literary means "religion or pious"! Why did Jina choose to use this term to describe something that is one of the constituents of this universe? We will try and find an answer to this question later in our discussion.

Adharma (medium of rest) The *Sutra* that describes this fifth substance of our universe is as under:

Just Like Dharma Substance, There Is Also An Adharma Substance. But The Difference Is That It Permits The Stability Of Jiva & Pudgal (Matter) In Universe In The Same Fashion As Earth Permits The Stability Of Objects Over It.
—*Samansuttam Sutra,* 634

This is an amazing substance. Its opposite of *Dharma* substance. *Dharma* permits other movable substances like matter to move around. This substance results in their getting stagnant at their respective place or orbits. What could be such a substance? To get a clue on what this substance is, let's get back to the *Sutra* above. Jina uses a simile to describe it for the ease of our understanding. It says that just as our planet Earth provides stability to the objects over it, similarly this substance gives stability to matter in the outer space. What is that mystical power which gives our planet this power? If we can find it, we will have an answer. And fortunately, we have already discovered it.

This discovery was made by one of the greatest genius of modern science. One day, as he was sitting under a tree in a garden, an apple fell over his head. This sparked a series of thoughts in his mind. He questioned why this apple fell on ground? He questioned why do every thing that we throws up in air tends to fall back? What is it that forces the objects to again and again get back to Earth? The genius was Newton and the answer to his questions was—Gravity.

Its gravity that gives stability to the objects on Earth. If our planet would not have this special force, then all the things on Earth would always be flying around. Its gravity that makes the objects stable.

Jina says the same force operates in this universe too and results in stability of all the matter that exists. All the starts, planets and moons! All the galaxies! And all the parallel universes! The name which Jina gives to this force is—*Adharma*—a force that results in stability of matter, and thus gives this universe, and its galaxies and planetary systems like our own Solar System; its specific shape and sphere of operation. If this force was non-existence, all the planets, stars and galaxies would be constantly on a move without any binding principle and thus constantly have been banging into each other creating a very chaotic situation. But gravity or *Adharma* as Jina calls it results in stoppage of this unorganized movement of matter and settles all the objects in their respective sphere of motion.

A question which again arises here is, why did Jina choose to name this force *Adharma*? This word literally means "non-religious" or "un-pious". Why did Jina choose such a negative term for a force that is the very source of stability of this universe? We will discover the answer to this question as we move ahead to discuss the sixth and the most mystical of all the six substances (*Dravya's*).

Jiva (**soul**) This sixth element or substance is *Jiva*. Until now all the five substances that we discussed have been proved scientifically to exist and be operational in our universe. But this sixth substance is something which our scientific community loves to disagree with. *Jiva* means soul—our real self. Jina says this soul is the sixth substance that constitutes this universe.

We have managed to gain a scientific understanding of all the balance five. Each of them exhibits a property that is unique to it, and differentiates it from the rest of the substances. *Akasha* (space) provides this universe a place where all other substances (*Drayas*) play. *Samay* (time) gives this universe a gauge where its changes and movements can be measured. *Pudgal* (matter) exhibits a unique property of fusion and fission and thus creates all the galaxies, stars, planets and rest everything that is visible in this universe.

Dharma (medium of motion) gives this universe a mean, where every thing that is movable can travel. *Adharma* (gravity) gives this universe stability and the required force to move around.

Each of these substances is unique and plays with other substances, but still keeps its distant characteristic intact. The same should be true for the last substance—the *Jiva*. It should also be independent of the rest of the substances and exhibit a characteristic that is distinctive to itself.

This property is consciousness. *Jiva* (soul) is capable of experiencing. It is capable of perceiving. None of the balance five substances has this property. They are neither aware of their own existence nor of others. Nor are they capable of attaining this experience. But *Jiva* is. It has this special characteristic that makes it capable of perception.

This *Jiva* interacts with *Pudgal* (matter) and takes a life form at places hospitable of cultivating life in our universe. From basic forms of life like amoeba to complex intelligent beings like humans, it manifests itself in every possible way in full glory. It is the presence of *Jiva* in bodies of various living forms that makes them capable of recognizing various experiences. Depending upon the capabilities of the living body they form, they become capable of experiencing pains and pleasures of this world. Say, for example, the being of amoeba is able to experience this existence from just one sense organ, whereas we humans are capable of experiencing the same existence from five sense organs.

This capability of the living forms to experience various emotions lasts only as long as the bond of body made of *Pudgal* (matter) and *Jiva* is intact. As soon as this bond breaks open, the body loses this property and is thus declared dead.

Such *Jivas* (souls), says Jina, are innumerable in number. And each is a sovereign in itself. As the material body it interacts with to create a life form withers off, it transcends it and takes another body, another form. And this process carries on.

During our discussion of *Dharma* (medium of motion), we raised a question that why did Jina prefer to use the word *Dharma* for the medium of motion. *Dharma* literally means religious or pious. What's pious in motion? I understand that this word was specifically used because the central subject for Jina is *Jiva* (soul) and its liberation from never-ending cycle of birth and rebirth in various life forms. The medium of motion that helps *Pudgal* (matter) move, also facilitates the motion of *Jiva* (soul) and thus permits it to move around in various life forms. This perhaps is the reason why this substance is called *Dharma*—the pious force or substance of universe.

Same perhaps is the reason why the medium of rest has been referred to as *Adharma* or impious one. Just as it traps the matter and forces it to get stationed in its specific orbit, similarly it forces the *Jiva* (soul) to get trapped in the gravity of objects of its respective desires and passions and keep revolving around them. This trap, this bond of attraction towards objects of passions prevents the natural movement of *Jiva* (soul) to higher planes and thus is called *Adharma*—the impious force.

This sixth substance called *Jiva* is central to the entire doctrine of Shraman school of thought. The aim of *Shraman* Theology is to create a structure, where this bond of *Adharma* that binds *Jiva* to the material objects could be humbled and thus permit it to take its natural course to *Moksha* (liberation).

This sixth substance is something, which still evades the science, and probably will continue to do so forever. This is because it can be seen and understood completely only by *Keveli*—someone who has reached the Thirteenth *Guna* we discussed above. So science will proably never ever be able to prove it with surety.

A question rose earlier that which of the two streams of Shraman School (Jainism or Buddhism) is better. The answer lies in our analysis of this sixth substance. Jain doctrine revolves around this sixth substance, while Buddhist doctrine denounces its existence. Rest everything is more or less same in the two traditions except for believe in existence of soul.

If, based on our analysis of the first five substances, we agree to give benefit of doubt to the existence of the sixth too; then the tradition which is suitable for us is—Jainism.

But if we are too much of an intellectual fundamentalist, and finds it difficult to believe in anything which can not be proved scientifically, then the path which is good for us is—Buddhism.

Both the traditions are tuned to help us break free from the forces of *Adharma* and settle us in *Dharma* so we can move ahead to our destined Godhood.

Comments are welcome.
Love
A Seeker Amit: email guidetogodhood@gmail.com
facebook: www.facebook.com/guidetogodhood.

Coming Up:
Guide to Godhood–II
The Making of a Buddha

In this volume, we will venture deeper into the *Sutras* of Shraman Theology. Here we will discover some of the most precious *Sutras* of Jina and contemplate over the same.

These *Sutras* were at their greatest height when Gautama was a young prince. Those were the days when Jina lived and preached. These *Sutras* must have reached His ears and become a catalyst in His renouncing the pleasures of His father's kingdom. These are the *Sutras* that lead to the "Making of the Buddha."

Epilogue

With this, we end this discussion on the Fourteen *Gunas*. This discussion was an attempt to explain to myself, the inherent meaning of the *Sutras* we discussed above. It was a result of an internal catharsis—a deep contemplation within; to discover the jewels of Shraman Theology.

In this process, I translated the original words of Jina—The Enlightened Master, took the liberty to contemplate over the same. And finally, in the discussion section, I tried to present my understanding to the various questions that often get raised when this topic is discussed.

It was indeed very childish for me to have attempted this. It reminds me of a *Sutra* from *Bhaktamar Stotra*:

Buddhya Vinapi Vibudharchit-Paadpeetha,
Stotum Samudyata Matirvigat-Trapo(a)ham.
Balam Vihay Jal-Sansthita Mindubimba
Manyah Ka Ichchhati Jinah Sahasa Graheetum?
(Just as a child attempts to hold the reflection of a moon in water,
Same way I have lost my senses as I am trying to write this *Sutra* for Someone, Whose throne is paid homage to by Demigods)

I feel the same as I look back at my work. Indeed it was very immature for me to have attempted to contemplate on the *Sutras* of someone, who's paid homage to by demigods. And definitely, there would have been mistakes that would have occurred in this process. I apologize for the same with folded hands and bowed forehead and seek the advice of the learned to help me correct the same.

Furthermore, in this process, if I erred in my under-standing, or have not translated the *Sutras* in the correct manner, or have merged any two *Sutras*, or have left any words of the *Sutras*, or have added any word on my own, or have left any section of the *Sutras*, or have not given the *Sutras* its due respect, or have not performed the correct translation, or have discussed *Sutras* that were not required to be discussed, or have left out *Sutras* that were required to be discussed, or have desired any personal gratifications in the process, or have contemplated on the *Sutras*, when it was not the right time to do so, or have not contemplated over them when it was the right time to do so, or have contemplated over the topics that were not required, or have not contemplated over the topics that were required to be contemplated upon, or while contemplating have performed any other mistake, then, again, with folded hands and bowed forehead, I sincerely apologize for the same and seek the advice of the learned to help me correct them.

Apart from taking the liberty to contemplate on the *Sutras* of Jina, I also took liberty to contemplate over the verses of various other religions, especially Buddhism, Christianity and Islam. It was a humble attempt to discover the similarities between various religions. In case I made any of the above mistakes in contemplating over these great theologies, or if I for any reason ended up not paying their Masters their due respect, then again, with folded hands and a bowed forehead sincerely apologize for the same and seek the advice of the learned to help me correct the same.

Micchami Dukkadam (with due apologies)
Sincerely,
A seeker—Amit

Notes

1. *Jina Sutra*, Osho. The Rebel Publishing House.
2. *Yoga: The Science of the Soul*, Osho. The Rebel Publishing House
3. *Britannica Encyclopedia*.
4. *Saman Suttam*, fourth edition, Sarv Seva Sangh Prakashan.
5. Anguttara Nikaya (online reference).
6. Shri Jain Divakar, *Samriti Grantha* (online reference).
7. Newspaper articles.
8. jainuniversity.org.
9. *The Secret of Secrets*, Osho. The Rebel Publishing House.
10. http://www.jainsamaj.org
11. Discovery Channel/National Geographic Channel/HISTORY CHANNEL.
12. *Mahavir Vani*, Osho.
13. Kunala Jatana (online reference).
14. http://www.palikanon.com/
15. Books I Have Loved (Oshobudhvihar.com.)
16. Sama . . . aphala Sutta: The Fruits of the Contemplative Life (online reference).
17. http://www.noble-buddhism-beliefs.com
18. http://bauswj.org – Mara and The Buddha.
19. http://www.worsleyschool.net/science/files/emc2/emc2.html
20. *The Universe in a Single Atom*, Broadway Books.
21. Wikipedia.
22. http://big-bang-theory.com/
23. http://skyserver.sdss.org/dr1/en/astro/universe/universe.asp
24. Ask Imam.com [12602] What is "chugli".
25. viewonbuddhism.org
26. *The Transformed Mind*.
27. discussion with pundits of Jainology.
28. *Ess Dhmmo Sanantano* (MP3 audio book).
30. o-meditation.com
31. www.srichinmoylibrary.com/books/1249/7/1/
32. *The Tattvasamgraha Sutra* (online reference).
33. The Guardian, Sunday 15 May 2011.
34. *Acharang Sutra* 2.6.
35. *Ekadhamma Suttas* (online reference).
36. *Godhika Sutta* (online reference).
37. *Jesus Lived in India*, Holger Kresten.

Notes

38. Rosicrucian Digest No2. 2007—Robert Geather.
39. http://essenes.net/index.php?Itemid=633&id=290&option=com_content&task=view
40. http://www.thenazareneway.com/therapeutae.html
41. *The Guardian*, Saturday 27 January 2007 by Aidan Rankin.
42. Baixares, Juan "Understanding: The Father Son Holy Spirit", http://www.geocities.com/athens/olympus/5257/4holispil.htm

Glossary

Acharya:	Head of various churches of Shraman tradition.
Adharma:	One of the six elementary substances (*Dravyas*) of our universe. It results in stability of the universe. Can be compared to gravity.
Agam:	Jain holy books.
Agathiya:	Non harming. Term used to collectively refer to the last four of bondages (*Karam-Bandh*) we create for ourselves by our actions.
Ahimsa:	Theory of live and let live. A non-violent way of leading life.
Ajatasattu:	Emperor of Magadha (current state of Bihar, India) in the days of Buddha
Ajeev:	Non-living. A term used to collectively refer to the first five *Dravyas* (elements).
Akasha:	Space. One of the six elementary substances (*Dravyas*) of our universe
Allah:	The name used to describe the Supreme God in Islam.
Alokakasha:	Non-universe. Space beyond the area of universe which contains all the matter.
Angas:	Jain holy books.
Anivrttikarna:	Ninth *Guna* (spiritual stage).
Anodri:	One of the *Tapas* (austerities) performed

Glossary

Anshan:	by Jains where they eat only minimal food. Fasting. Is one of the Tapas (austerities) performed by Jains.
Antaraya Karma:	One of the eight type of bandages we create for ourselves (*Karam-Bandh*). Collectively, they are referred to actions we do which create obstacles for other creatures.
Anter-Atman:	*Anter* means inside and Atman means soul. Thus, *Anter-Atman* is a being or soul who is settled in itself and have cut short the bonds of desires and passions of the outside world.
Anter-mhurhat:	Time span of forty-eight minutes.
Apramat Virakt:	Seventh *Guna* (spiritual stage).
Apurvakarana:	Eighth *Guna* (spiritual stage).
Ara:	A huge span of time with specific characteristics that our planet passes through as our universe revolves
Arati:	Improper behavior
Arihant:	The Being who has annihilated four of a total of eight bonds which bind a soul in the transmigratory cycle. Such beings gets liberated and become *Siddha*—the God after death by annihilating the balance four bonds in this life span itself.
Artha-sastra:	An ancient Indian treatise on statecraft, economics and military strategy written by Kautilya popularly known as Chanakya.
Asata-Vedniya:	Pain giving actions we bind for ourselves by giving pain to others.
Ashrav:	Creation of new bondages as we perform our actions (*Karmic* influx).
Atmic Cycle:	Sum total of all the lives a being has lived in various forms of lives.

Avirata Samyag Drishti:	Fourth *Guna* (spiritual stage).
Avsarpani:	That phase of *Kala-Chakra* where our planet experiences constant erosion of resources resulting in ever-increasing pain for humans. Our planet is currently passing through this phase of its *Kala-Chakra* (Regressive Half Cycle).
Ayogi Keveli Jin:	Fourteenth *Guna* (spiritual stage).
Ayushya Karma:	Actions we perform that result in deciding our age in the next life.
Bahir-Atman:	Bahir means outward and Atman means soul. *Bahir-Atman* means a soul or being obsessed with material world.
Bhagwaan:	Name used to describe The Supreme Soul—*Param-Atman* by Hindus, Buddhist and Jains.
Bhaya:	Fear.
Bikkhu:	A Shraman monk.
Bodhicitta:	Infinite altruism. A state of mind that desires well-being of all sentient beings.
Brahma:	The name used to describe The Supreme God in Hinduism.
Carvaka:	A sect of atheist in ancient India who denounced the existence of God and of soul. They rubbished all established religions of the time.
Charkas:	Energy centers of our body as per Tantric and yogic traditions.
Darshana-varaniya Karma:	The actions which result in limiting our ability to see and comprehend the things as they are. Vision obscuring actions. One of the eight bondages we create for

Glossary

	ourselves by our actions.
Desh Virakt:	Fifth *Guna* (spiritual stage).
Dev-gati:	Heavenly after-life.
Devta:	A demigod.
Dharma:	One of the six elementary substances (*Dravyas*) of our universe. It helps in movement of matter and soul in the universe. Can be compared to dark matter. Also called *Dharmastakiye*.
Dharmastikaye:	Also popularly referred to as *Dharma*, is one of the six elementary substances (*Dravyas*) of the universe. It's a force that makes matter and souls move around.
Dravya:	Those elementary substances of the universe which are eternal and independent of each other. These are a total of six in number.
Dwesha:	Term used to collectively referrer to negative human emotions like envy, hate and aversion.
Eik-Indriya Jiva:	Eik means one. Indriya means sense organ and Jiva means soul. This term is used to describe the beings capable of experiencing this universe with just one sense organ, i.e. body (touch).
Ghatiya:	Harming. Term used to collectively refer to the first four of the eight type of bondages we create for ourselves by our actions (*Karam-Bandh*).
Gotra Karma:	Actions which result in deciding the type of family we will be born in our next life.
Guna:	Spiritual stage of a being. Total fourteen in number.
Hasya:	Actions that result in ridiculing another person.

Himsa:	Violence. Act of harming another living creature.
Indra:	The king of heaven.
Ishwar:	A name used to describe the Supreme God in Hinduism.
Jananavaraniya Karma:	Actions which result in reducing our ability to gain knowledge. Knowledge obscuring actions.
Jati-Samran-Gyan:	Knowledge of past life or multiple lives.
Jeev:	A living creature.
Jeeveshna:	Desire to live and consume (*bhoga*).
Jin:	The conqueror. Term used to describe the one who has conquered his vices.
Jina:	Term used to describe Bhagwaan Mahavira—the twenty-fourth and the last great master of Shraman Tradition. It means the conqueror (of vices).
Jiva:	Soul.
Jugupsa:	Disgustful behavior.
Kala:	Time.
Kala-Chakra:	Time taken by our universe to revolve completely around its central mountain (*Parvat*).
Karam-Bandh:	Bondage of our past actions, total of eight in number.
Karma:	Action and the after-effect of a past Action referred to as *Karam-Bandh*.
Katha-Upanishad:	One of the *Upanishad* (an ancient Indian text).
Kautalya:	A noted statesman of ancient India and teacher of Emperor Chandra Gupta Maurya. He wrote the treatise *Arthasastra*.
Kenopanishad:	One of the *Upanishad* (an ancient Indian text).

Glossary

Keveli:	State of Godhood.
Krodha:	Anger.
Kshapak:	One of the directions taken by a being after it reaches the seventh *Guna* (spiritual stage). Following this direction, a being completely annihilates his past actions.
Kshin Moh:	Twelfth *Guna* (spiritual stage).
Kundalini:	The home of our vital energies as per Yogic and Tantric traditions.
Lobha:	Greed
Lokaksha:	That part of our universe which contains all the matter & soul.
Magdha:	Name of a kingdom in Ancient India in the current state of Bihar.
Mahayana:	One of the branches of Buddhism.
Mana:	Pride.
Mantra:	A small hymn or prayer. Often supposed to have special powers.
Mara:	Term used for Satan in Buddhism. The evil side of our brain.
Maya:	Deceitful behaviour.
Meneka:	Name of a nymph in Indian mythology.
Meru:	A massive cosmic structure (*Parvat*) in the center of our universe. Its massive size imparts it gravity which makes our universe and all the other parallel universes which exist out there to revolve around.
Minotaur:	A mythical Greek character that was half man and half bull.
Misra-bhava:	Third *Guna* (spiritual stage).
Mithyatva:	First *Guna* (spiritual stage).
Mohiniya Karma:	Those actions which result in creating desires and passions in us. Deluding actions. These are one of the eight type

	of bondages we create for ourselves (*Karam-Bandh*).
Moksha:	Release from the cycle of transmigration of soul.
Nachiketa:	A legendary child referred to in *Katha-Upanishad* who is told about soul and Brahma and the relationship between the two by Yama—the king of death.
Nama Karma:	The actions which result in type of form (body/color/features, etc.) we will get in our next life.
Namokar Mantra:	A prayer paying homage to the souls who have attained Godhood and are on the path to attaining Godhood.
Narak-gati:	Hellish after-life.
Nigoda:	In Jain tradition, its the state of a soul which is completely opposite to the state of *Moksha*. At *Moksha* a soul escapes the cycle of transmigration and at Nigoda, its entrapped in this state so throughly that its unable to make any effort on its own to escape the cycle of transmigration. In this state, the being lives in the form of an *Eik-Indriya-Jiva* (beings with just one sense organ).
Nirgranth:	Knot-less. Term used to describe someone who has completely detached itself from knots of desires.
Nirjara:	One of the nine *Tatvas*. symbolizes release from past actions (*Karam-Bandh*).
Nisang:	Desire-less.
Panch-Indriya Jiva:	Panch means five. *Indriya* means sense organ and *Jiva* means soul. This term is used to describe the beings capable of experiencing this universe with all the five

	sense organ, i.e. body, eyes, ears, nose and tongue.
Papa:	One of the nine *Tatvas*. Symbolizes the bad actions we have bonded ourselves to that we will need to reap in future.
Param-Atman:	*Param* means supreme and *Atman* means soul. *Param-Atman* means a soul or a being who has completely annihilated all desires and passions of the material world and has thus conquered all His vices completely.
Parmanu:	Smallest portion which the matter can be broken into.
Patanjali:	Father of Indian tradition of Yoga.
Pragya:	Intellect.
Pramat Virakt:	Sixth *Guna* (spiritual stage).
Pratikarman:	A special Jain prayer performed to apologize for the misdeeds.
Pudgal:	Matter.
Punya:	One of nine *Tatvas*. Symbolizes the good actions we have bonded ourselves too which shall bear benefits for us in future.
Purvas:	Ancient Jain texts.
Raga:	Term used to collectively refer to positive human emotions like love, admiration and attachments.
Rati:	Prejudiced behaviour.
Sadhavi:	A nun who has cut short her desires and passions by accepting the Five Great (*Panch-maha-vrata*) vows.
Sadhu:	The monk who has cut short his desires and passions by accepting the Five Great (*Panch maha-vrata*) vows.
Samadhi:	A state of deep meditation.
Saman Suttam:	A Jain holy book compiled by joint efforts of monks of all the major churches of Jain

	tradition at request of Acharya Vinoba.
Samkit:	A state of mind of a being at the fourth *Guna* (spiritual stage).
Samsara:	Cycle of repeated birth and death.
Samvar:	Stoppage of performance of new actions. One of the nine *Tatvas*.
Samvatsari:	Most auspicious day of Shraman Jains celebrated at the fiftieth day of start of rainy season to commemorate the start of human civilization in the current phase of *Kala-Chakra*.
Samyag Chariter:	Samyag means right and *Chariter* means character. *Samyag Chariter* thus means right character. Collectively, it's referred to the changes in character of a person when he starts using the formulae of *Tatvas* to his benefit.
Samyag Darshan:	Samyag means right and Darshan means vision. Samyag Darshan means the right vision about God, soul and working of this universe. Its understanding the fact why we are what we are and what we can do to alter our destiny. Its one of the three gems of Shraman tradition.
Samyag Drishti:	Someone who has achieved *Samyag Darshan* (Right Vision).
Sangha:	The commune.
Sanyam:	Self restrain to avoid doing those actions which result in bondages (*Karam-Bandh*) resulting in miseries in future. A state of mind which is achieved as a result of understanding of *Tatvas*.
Sasvadana:	Second *Guna* (spiritual stage)
Sata-Vedniya:	Pleasure giving actions we bind for ourselves as a result of giving happiness

Glossary

Satan:	to others. The evil one in Jews, Christians and Islam who initiates the person into actions which lead him away from God.
Sayogi Keveli Jin:	Thirteenth *Guna* (spiritual stage).
Shok:	Sorrow.
Shradha:	Faith.
Shradhan:	Intellectual analysis of a subject.
Shraman:	An ancient Indian tradition. Buddhism and Jainism are an off-shoots of this tradition.
Shravak:	A lay male follower of Shraman tradition.
Shravika:	A lay female follower of Shraman tradition.
Siddha:	Name used to describe the Supreme God in Shraman religion.
Sthanak:	The holy place of Swetambera Jains where their monks and nuns stay for brief periods. Its also the assembly point of lay followers of this tradition.
Sthavar Jeev:	Immovable beings like plants.
Sthulabhadra:	Head of the Jain Church (*Acharya*) under whose guidance the *Sutras* of Jina were first compiled as a manuscript.
Sufi:	A mystical sect of Islam that got extremely popular in India mainland due to their close similarity to Indian mysticism.
Suksham Sampray:	Tenth *Guna* (spiritual stage).
Sutra:	A small verse of a sacred book.
Swami:	Master of oneself.
Swastika:	Ancient Indian symbol which symbolizes the movement of soul.
Swetambera:	A Jain sect.
Tapas:	Techniques of taming one's mind, body and thoughts so internal energies could

	be harnessed.
Tatvas:	The centre most knowledge of Jain Theology.
Tirthankara:	Term used to describe Great Masters (Prophets) of Shraman tradition.
Tras Jeev:	Mobile living beings
Triyanch-gati:	Afterlife that results in our birth as an animal, insect or a plant.
Upadhaya:	The being so thoroughly established in the pious forces of *Dharmastikaye* (*Dharma*) that they can preach others on the same.
Upsham:	suppression of desires or actions.
Upshant Moh:	Eleventh *Guna* (spiritual stage).
Utsarpani:	That phase of *Kala-Chakra* where our planet experiences constant increase of resources resulting in ever-increasing pleasure for humans (Progressive half cycle).
Vajrayana:	A sect of Buddhism.
Vanyik:	A state of blind faith. A type of *Mithyatva*.
Veda:	Desire for sex.
Vedniya Karma:	The actions that we bind for ourselves as a result of giving pain or pleasures to others.
Vihar:	A place where Shraman monks and nuns reside and move around to beg for alms.
Vit-ragi:	*Vit* means transcendence and *Rag* means subtle bonds of attachment. Vit-ragi is a term used to describe someone who has transcended all attachments and thus experiences neither positive human emotions of love, nor negative human emotions like envy or hatred.

Index

Abhigrahik Mithyatva 41–42, 44–46, 52
Acharya 1, 25, 29, 159
Acharya Vinoba 160
Adharma 161, 166, 173–76
Agam 160
Agathiya 99, 156
Agyan 40
Ahimsa 76, 80, 89, 131, 159
Ajatasattu 110
Ajeev 43, 57, 64, 66
Akasha 168–69
Alexander 74
Allah 3–5, 25, 44, 50
Anataraya Karma 97–98
Andromeda galaxy 165
Anguttara Nikaya 43
Anhad Naad 109
Anivsttikarma 31, 33, 118
Anodri 140
Anubhava 6, 71, 73
Anshan 141
Anter Atman 1, 11–12, 24
Anter-mhurhat 117
Anubhuti 71–73
Apramat Virakat 31, 33, 93, 111, 121, 129
Apurvakarana 31, 33, 109–10, 120
Ara 162
Arahatship 98
Arati 99
Arihant 1, 25–29, 53, 156–57

Aristotle, 148
Arthasastra (Handbook of Profit) 7
Aryans 78
Asata-vedniya 101
Ashrav 58, 61–66
Atman 32
Atmic Cycle 32, 34, 45, 51, 55, 69–70, 98, 105, 109, 126, 129
Avidhya 40
Avirata Samyag Drishti 31, 33, 51, 69–70, 98, 158
Avsarpani 162
Ayogi Keveli Jin 31, 33, 153
Ayushya Karma 99–100, 156

Bhagwaan 11
Bahir Atman 1, 11–12
Bhaya 98
Bible 22–23, 26
Big Bang Theory 14–15, 163
Bodhicitta 133
Bodhisattva 133
Brahma 4–5, 7, 25

Carvaka 6–7, 10
Chinese Tao 110
Christian Trinity 150
CIA 113
Cold War 112–13
Creator of His Own Destiny 9

Dalai Lama 89, 133

Dark Matter 170
Darshana-vararya Karma 96
Darwin 123
Day of the Judgment 1
Desh Virakt 31, 33, 83–84, 92, 130, 158
Dev-gati 59–60
Devta 11
Dharma 22–25, 29, 133, 161, 166, 170–72, 174–76
Dharmastikaye 22, 166
Dravya 16, 161, 166, 168–69, 173
Dwesha 64

Eikant Vaad 40
Eik-Indriya Jiva 10, 32
Ellis, F.R. George 14
Essence and Nazarenes 137, 149
Extra Sensory Perception (ESP) 112–15

Ghatiya 99
Gotra Karma 100
Guna 31, 33–35, 37, 54, 62, 64, 71, 83, 88–89, 95–97, 99, 101–2, 104–5, 111, 113–14, 118, 130, 139, 156, 175

Hasya 99
Hawking, Stephen 7
Himsa 80
Hitler 74, 76–77, 79
Hubble, Edwin 164

Indris 127
Ishwar 3–5, 7
Isigili Mountain 98

Jain theology 16, 54, 117, 129–30, 168
Jananavaraniya 95

Jati-Samran-Gyan 110–11
Jeev 56–57, 64–65
Jeevashna 8, 24
Jhana 98
Jiva 43, 141, 173–75
Jin 157
Jina 11–13, 36, 45, 51–54, 65, 69, 80, 84, 88–89, 102, 107, 125–26, 130–31, 138, 140–43, 147, 150, 158–59, 167, 170–75
Jugupsa 99
Jyatti 16

Kafir 45
Kala 169
Kala-Chakra 144, 156, 160–63, 165–66
Karam Bandh 58, 61, 94–95, 99, 101–2, 104
Karma 19–20, 31, 47, 53, 56, 59–61, 64–67, 93–94, 96–101, 107, 120, 145, 156
Katha Upanishad 12
Kautilya 7
Kenopanishad 4
Keveli 157, 175
Khan, Changez 75–76
Kingdom of God 6
Krodha 98
Kshapak 101–2, 104, 129
Kshin Moh 31, 33, 130, 153

Lankavatara Sutra 133
Lao-Tzu 112–13
Lemaitre, Georges 164
Lokakasha 168
Lokayat 6
Lobha 99

Mahaparinirvana Sutra 132

Index

Mahayana 134
Mana 99
Mantra 27, 53
Mara 99, 128–29
Marx, Karl 6
Maya 99
Microsoft 41
Misra-bhava 31, 33, 51, 98
Mithya 127
Mithyatva 31, 33, 39–42, 44, 46, 51–52, 54, 67, 69–70, 95–98, 120
Moh 98, 129
Mohiniya Karma 95, 98
Moksha 12, 14, 16–17, 24, 26, 29, 31, 33–35, 54, 65, 103, 110, 153, 157, 163, 175
Mukti 157

Nama Karma 100
Namokar Mantra 28–29, 53
Nanak gati 59–60
Napolean 74
Nazis 78
New Testament 118
Nigoda 17–18
Nile 148
Nirgranth 154–56
Nirvana 12, 26–27, 29, 31, 33, 65–66, 103, 110, 153, 157, 159, 163
Nisang 155–56
Nostradamus 112
Notovitch, 131–32, 135–37, 149–50

Old Testament 119, 148

Panch Indriya Jiva 10, 32
Papa 58, 61, 64, 66
Param-Atman 1, 11–12

Parmanu 167–68
Parvat 161–62
Patanjali 109–12, 118
Philo 138–42, 144–48
Pramana 6
Pramat Virakt 31, 33, 91, 121
Pratikarman 145, 147
Prayga 37, 105–6
Pudgal 57, 167–68, 170, 173–75
Punya 58, 61, 64, 66
Purvas 159–60

Qur'an 2

Raga 64
Rati 99
Rising of Kundalini 109
Robin, Vera 170

Saccatapavi 122
Sadhavi 141
Sadhu 25, 29, 141
Samadhi 109
Saman Sutra 32. 92, 160
Samkit 69, 83, 88
Samsara 91, 157
Samvar 64, 66, 103, 163
Samvatsari 144, 147
Samyag Chariter 71
Sangha 34, 36–37
Sanyag Darshan 12, 71
Sanyag Drishti 142
Sanyam 139
Satan 24, 99, 127–28
Sata-Vednaiya 101
Sasvadana 31, 33, 46
Sayogi Keveli Jin 31, 33, 153, 156
Secrates 45
Seydel, Rudolf 151
Shok 98

Shraddha 104
Shradhan 104
Shraman 8–10, 12–17, 19–29, 32, 34, 37, 52–55, 61, 72–73, 76, 80, 87, 89, 92, 94, 96, 100, 105–6, 112–13, 121, 126, 130, 132, 134–35, 137–39, 143–45, 147–48, 151, 156, 158, 161, 163–64, 166, 175
Shravak 146–47
Shravika 146–47
Siddha 1, 14, 26–29, 53, 65
Socrates 45
Sthanak 146
Sthavar Jeev 73, 84
Sufi 3–5, 47, 50
Suksham Sampray 31, 33, 120, 124
Super Man 75, 78
Supreme Entity 2–3
Sutra 4, 12–13, 32, 39, 47, 70, 72–74, 84–85, 87, 92–93, 95, 103, 107, 109–11, 118–21, 125–26, 130–31, 133, 135–36, 142, 150, 154–55, 158, 160, 170–72
Swami 84
Swastika 59–60, 65–66

Tapas 140–41
Tatvas 46, 52, 54–56, 58, 61–67, 69, 71, 88, 91, 103–4, 107, 163
The Last Mind 126, 128, 130
Theory of Evolution 123
Thera Godhika 97–98
Therapeutae 137, 141–42, 149
Therapeutrides 141
Tibetan Buddhist School 131
Tirthankara 13, 27, 53
Tras Jeev 73, 84
Triyanch gati 59–60

Upadhaya 25, 29
Upsham 101, 104, 122
Upshant Moh 31, 33, 124, 129
Utopia 55
Utsarpani 162
Ultimate weapon 113

Vajrayana 134
Vanyik 41
Veda 6, 136
Vedniya Karma 100
Vihar 13
Viprit gayan 42
Vitragi 28

WHO 125
Windows Vista 42

YHVH 1, 25

Definition of God

Fourteen Guna's—The Path

Stages of Mithyatva—The Legacy of Our Animalistic Past

Arrival of Samkit—The Blossoming of Humanity

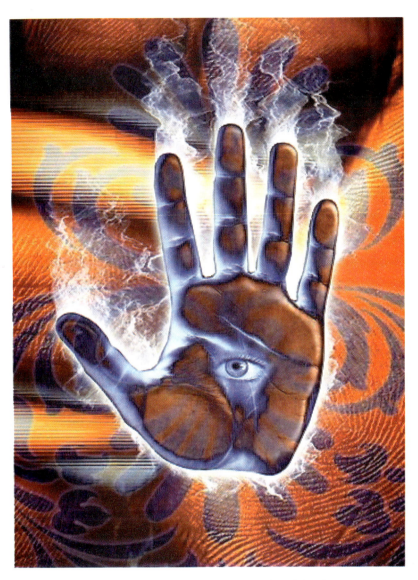

Stepping into Desh Virakt—Declaration of Freedom

State of Shramanhood—The Boarding Pass to Godhood

Experiences of Apurvakarana—Arrival of ESPs

Anter-mhurhat—Last Forty-eight Minutes to Godhood

Keveli—The State of Godhood